Word o

MARTIN KITCHEN is a graduate in modern languages and theology of the University of London and holds a doctorate in New Testament Studies from the University of Manchester. He prepared for ordination at King's College, London, and with the Southwark Ordination Course and is a Residentiary Canon of Durham Cathedral.

GEORGIANA HESKINS teaches Religious Studies at Eltham College, an independent school for boys in south east London. She is a priest-vicar at Southwark Cathedral and lives in the Borough of Greenwich, within sight of the Thames Barrier and the Millennium Dome. She was, until recently, Tutor at the South East Institute for Theological Education where she taught Pastoral and Biblical Studies. Her own preparation for ordination was at King's College, London, and at Westcott House in Cambridge, and most of her preaching experience has been gained in London.

STEPHEN MOTYER spent some years at the pulpit-face trying to make the lectionary live in rural Hertfordshire, before taking up his present post as New Testament Lecturer at London Bible College. Before that he taught at Oak Hill College, and looks back with thankfulness on theological studies at Cambridge, Bristol, Tübingen and London. With the other authors of this Commentary, he shares a vision for inspiring preaching at the heart of worship.

Also by the same authors:

Word of Promise – A commentary on the Lectionary readings, Year A

Word of Life – A commentary on the Lectionary readings, Year C

Word of Truth

A Commentary on the Lectionary Readings for the Principal Service on Sundays and Major Holy Days

Year B

Martin Kitchen,
Georgiana Heskins and Stephen Motyer

CANTERBURY
PRESS
Norwich

© Martin Kitchen, Georgiana Heskins and Stephen Motyer, 1999
First published in 1999 by The Canterbury Press Norwich
(a publishing imprint of Hymns Ancient & Modern Limited,
a registered charity)
St Mary's Works, St Mary's Plain,
Norwich, Norfolk, NR3 3BH

British Library Cataloguing in Publication Data

A catalogue record for this book is available
from the British Library

ISBN 1-85311-317-4

Typeset by Rowland Phototypesetting,
Bury St Edmunds, Suffolk
Printed in Great Britain by
Biddles Ltd, Guildford and King's Lynn

Contents

Preface

The present volume of commentary on the readings for the Sundays and Principal Feast Days of the Christian year will see the reader through the greater part of the first year of the new millennium, as some see it, or the final year of the present one as a stricter calendar understanding would designate it. That it should be edited within yards of the tomb of The Venerable Bede, in Durham, is appropriate, for he played a major part in popularizing the marking of time from the birth of Jesus, which he took to be in the year 1 *Anno Domini*. This was a departure from the contemporary practice of dating events from the birth of secular rulers.

The relationship between Christian tradition and the start of the millennium is ambiguous. The date is wrong, and this is not 'the 2,000th birthday of Jesus'. There never was a time when he did not exist; and his eternal life in God and in the church cannot be dated, for age does not weary Jesus who rose from the dead. Nevertheless this is a useful point at which to remind ourselves that Christian discipleship takes the passage of time seriously, for it takes the whole of life seriously, and the time of life passes 'like a watch in the night'. These comments on the Lectionary are offered to the churches in the hope that they will help Christian people to reckon that their daily walk with God may be informed by thoughtful and prayerful consideration of the scriptures. We who have written them are convinced of the vitality of Christ in the world and we pray, both that preachers may be inspired by our reflections to work further on the texts themselves, and that regular churchgoers will make use of these thoughts. They might read them to prepare themselves for worship or, once Sunday worship is passed, they might study them to aid further reflection on the biblical texts.

It has been a pleasure to produce them, even amid the demands of busy pastoral and teaching responsibilities; Georgiana Heskins,

Stephen Motyer and I have been happy to work together again, and Christine Smith of the Canterbury Press has shown remarkable patience. Our families and colleagues have again proved supportive and understanding, and we would wish to record our thanks to them.

MARTIN KITCHEN
Durham
Pentecost 1999

Introduction

On Reading St Mark's Gospel

Word of Truth gains its title from one of the emphases of the Gospel according to St Mark, which is adopted for serial reading in Year B. This Gospel is probably one of the most significant texts in the literature of the West. If that sounds an excessive claim to make for a slight work (it takes up barely more than twenty pages in an average, two-column edition of the New Testament), then we should recall that, in all likelihood, this is the earliest piece of writing we have which tells any story of Jesus of Nazareth.

Earliest commentary on Mark thought that this Gospel was simply an abbreviated version of that attributed to St Matthew, in spite of the fact that there was a tradition that the testimony of St Peter lay behind it. However, when literary dependence between the Gospels was noticed, it was first assumed that the evident priority of Mark must mean that it was more 'historical'; the paragraphs which go to make up the Gospel's structure have a brief and pithy tone to them, and the use which both Matthew and Luke make of Mark indicate that considerable freedoms were taken with the text. However, the work of Wilhelm Wrede gave the lie to that view, for he identified the literary device of the 'Messianic Secret', that is, the theme that runs throughout the Gospel that Jesus does not wish his identity as the Christ, or Son of God, to be broadcast. St Mark's Gospel is therefore a conscious piece of writing, and, indeed, according to the American critic Harold Bloom, the Jesus of Mark's Gospel is one of the great characters of literary culture.

What characterizes this story of Jesus are his parables, his 'mighty acts', the conflict with the contemporary authorities that led to his death and the consequent set of questions as to his identity. None of these is without its problems. His parables may form the basis, not only of much folk wisdom but also of moral argument down the centuries, but in themselves they are highly self-conscious creations, capable of several layers of meaning, and central to Jesus's focusing of the concept of 'the kingdom of God'. His 'powerful acts' – misleadingly read as 'miracles' – stand as symbols, both of divine compassion and of the same 'kingdom' of which the parables are the allusive rhetoric.

The conflict which contributed to the brevity of his life might be a model for tragedy – it has been pointed out that, for all that the general consensus is that the active life and 'ministry' (if that is the right word) of Jesus lasted for about three years, the events of St Mark's Gospel may be encompassed within the period of about nine months. Conflict with the Jewish authorities begins early in the story, and it culminates in his crucifixion. One commentator has suggested that the Gospels are 'passion narratives with extended introductions'. Though such a view is patently false, it does draw attention to the fact that, in the early period of the church's life, 'to be a Christian', one commentator has said, 'was to have taken up a certain attitude to Christ's death and his resurrection, rather than to his mighty works or his teaching'.

Who Jesus was and who he is remain a puzzle, and theological formulae do not explain it; they simply sketch the parameters of the problem. The Gospel opens with quotations from prophecies in the Hebrew scriptures which are taken to refer to John the Baptizer, who will come 'to prepare the way of the Lord', that is, God. But it is Jesus who comes, to be baptized by John in the river Jordan. If his identity is to be discovered from his relationships, then it is with the God of contemporary Jewish worship that his primary relationship consists. Jesus addresses him as 'Abba' (an intimate, though adult, term) in Mark 14:36. His overriding passion is God's kingdom, which is the fact and reality of God's kingship in the life of his people.

The next relationship is that which he has, not with his family, which is strangely distant – as Mark 3:31ff. indicates – but with the disciples whom he calls and who follow him on his travels. They share his life, they (appear to) serve his needs, they listen to his parables and the explanations of them (such as they are) and they ask questions of him. Mostly, it may be said, they perform the function of listeners to his stories and witnesses of his actions. It is they, rather than he, who are faced with the question of his identity. Indeed, they have little significance apart from him, as though their own identity depended solely upon their estimate of him.

It is at this point that the status of Mark as a conscious piece of writing rears its head again. Readers are invited – required, almost – to enter the story, to hear the parables, to witness the actions. It is to them that the question is put concerning who he is, and it is as they face the question concerning him that they discover something of who they are themselves.

Moreover the question is urgent. There is no escaping the breathless pace of this Gospel; the word 'immediately' is one of its favourites; and this has implications for the way it is read. The demands it seems to make for a radical discipleship are written into its structure; the beginning is a curious mixture of allusion and event, and at the end the women at the tomb, after being sent back to Galilee by the young man inside the tomb, say nothing to anyone, 'for they were afraid'. This seems to send the reader her- or himself back to the beginning where the whole story started, as if the end really is, in T. S. Eliot's words, 'where we start from'.

We are confronted with the possibility that the truth which is really at stake is not merely that which can be conveyed in propositions, or in stories, or even in a story comprising the telling of stories; rather it is that which is focused primarily in knowledge of a person.

Word of Truth

The First Sunday of Advent

Isaiah 64:1–9
Psalm 80:1–7, 17–19
1 Corinthians 1:3–9
Mark 13:24–37

O VER 2,500 years have passed since Isaiah 64 was written, but it could have been yesterday. All around the prophet sees sin, uncleanness and people destroying themselves by their wickedness. He longs for God to intervene, to 'rend the heavens and come down' (v. 1). The prophet associates himself with all this sin: notice the 'we' in verses 5–9. At their best, this is what God's people have always done; they do not sit in judgment on the horrors of this world, but confess them as if 'we' ourselves were responsible for them. After all, we belong to the human race which has so wantonly wrecked God's beautiful world, by gnawing at it in ghastly self-destructive greed. Can we stand back from the vileness we see around? It is particularly appropriate that at the Eucharist we should bear a suffering and sinful world on our hearts in repentance before God.

The constant expectation of the Bible is that God will come, to judge the world and redeem his people. Wrong will be righted, the wreckers brought to book, and God's plan to save the world will be completed. In the New Testament, the coming of God becomes the coming of Jesus, as we see from the 1 Corinthians reading. It is hard to overestimate the significance of the 'second coming' of Christ within the New Testament. This brief passage from Paul gives a taste of the way in which, for him, the future 'revealing' or 'appearance' of Jesus formed the essential horizon of the Christian life – 'the end' towards which we work, prepare ourselves, and direct our whole existence. Is this still a credible belief in the twenty-first century? 'Apocalyptic' language like that in today's Gospel does not fit well with a modern scientific outlook, which tells us that stars cannot 'fall from heaven'. But this should not put us off, because we need to look behind the language and to ask why the New Testament writers – and Jesus himself –

3

insisted on this 'end' towards which the world is steaming. The answer emerges from the whole of Mark 13, from which our Gospel is taken. Here we see three things, all of vital importance for our Christian message today.

First, the Presence of God. God is not distant from his world, but knows it. This is implied simply by the predictions that Jesus makes. Ultimately, though torn by war and suffering, the world rests in God's hands; and when dreadful, abominable evil occurs, 'Watch out!' Jesus tells his disciples, 'the judgment of God is at hand' (vv. 14ff.). Because God is involved with his world, there must be an 'end' (v. 13).

Second, the Proclamation of the Gospel. If we ask, 'Why doesn't God act in judgment now? The world is so evil!', the answer of Mark 13 is, because God wants to save the world, rather than judge it, and there must be time for the gospel to be preached to all nations (v. 10). However, for the same reason, there must one day be final salvation, ultimate deliverance from sin and suffering for a damaged world.

Third, the Coming of God's Son. This is the focus of the last part of the chapter, our Gospel. The 'Son of Man' comes to put into effect the judgment and deliverance that God plans for his world. Whatever happens to the heavenly bodies, this is the world's horizon, and we need to be ready (vv. 33–37).

★   ★   ★

The Second Sunday of Advent

Isaiah 40:1–11
Psalm 85:1–2, 8–13
2 Peter 3:8–15a
Mark 1:1–8

THE readings for this Sunday and next focus on John the Baptist, that strange prophetic figure who caused such a stir in Judea in the mid-twenties CE. Initially, he remained as large in Jewish memory as Jesus; the Jewish historian Josephus, writing about fifty years later, tells the story of his execution by Herod, and writes that 'he was a good man, who told the Jews to practise virtue, to conduct their relationships with each other with faithfulness and reverence towards God, and thus to come together in baptism'. Josephus adds that great crowds gathered to hear him, 'for they were deeply stirred when they heard his words'. But Josephus does not mention the most vital thing about John, that he saw himself as the 'voice' mentioned in Isaiah 40:3, announcing the coming of the Lord himself and seeking to 'prepare his way'.

The picture in Isaiah is the coming of a mighty King, on a royal progress around his dominions. A road has to be built ahead of his arrival, levelling the hills and filling the valleys, smoothing out the 'rough places' so that 'the glory of the Lord shall be revealed' (Isaiah 40:4–5). In the first century, many Jews were expecting a 'coming' of the Lord like this. Generally speaking, they thought of this 'coming' in political terms: the Lord would arrive, rescue Israel from the power of Rome, overthrow all her enemies, and set up a new kingdom in Jerusalem, one of peace and prosperity. After years of insecurity, Israel would at last be safe. John, however, introduces a new, and unusual, note into his proclamation of the 'coming' of the Lord. God will come, not to deal with Israel's enemies, but to transform Israel herself. 'Repent!' John cries, urging people to be ready for the Lord, and offering baptism as a sign of their deep-seated 'confession' of sin (v. 5). Then the reason for this need for moral preparation appears: when the Lord comes, 'he will baptize you with the Holy Spirit' (v. 8). What did this expectation mean for John? His fellow-Jews had been looking forward to the ultimate punch-up, God versus their enemies. John knew that the coming of God was a dangerous prospect. The parallel in Matthew to this passage (Matthew 3:7–10) makes clear his expectation of judgment on all who 'presume to say to themselves, "We have Abraham as our Father"'. Blithe confidence that God would judge the sins of Israel's enemies, and ignore Israel's sins, was completely misplaced. What was needed was radical repentance, preparing for radical cleansing through the 'baptism' of the Holy Spirit.

As we approach the festival of the incarnation we must remind ourselves of the purpose of this amazing 'coming of God' in human flesh. He came to make us holy, that is, to restore the full capacity of intimate fellowship between us and himself. To be 'baptized with the Holy Spirit' is the ultimate symbol and seal of that relationship, the greatest hope for all on earth – and the Pentecost birthright of all who belong to Christ.

★   ★   ★

The Third Sunday of Advent

Isaiah 61:1–4, 8–11
Psalm 126 *or* Luke 1:47–55
1 Thessalonians 5:16–24
John 1:6–8, 19–28

OUR second meditation on John the Baptist focuses on the statement in John 1:7, 'he came as a witness'. John sees himself simply as a Voice, crying out in the wilderness, bearing testimony to the Light. We are paradoxical creatures, we human beings. On the one hand, we rejoice in believing that we are wonderfully valuable – we must be, or the Son of God would not have thought us worth dying for. On the other hand, however, we persist in believing that we don't exist for ourselves, and that our value lies in what we may be and do for Someone Else, not for ourselves.

John shows us this paradox. On the one hand he was clearly a powerful, even unique human being. He prompted a high-level delegation from Jerusalem to investigate him (John 1:19), the members of which clearly expected him to make dramatic claims for himself (at least 'Elijah', or 'the prophet', if not 'the Christ'!). Jesus himself commented that 'among those born of women no one has arisen greater than John the Baptist' (Matthew 11:11). Greater than Abraham, Moses, Elijah . . . John was great indeed.

6

On the other hand, however, he was only a Voice, bearing witness to Someone Else. His whole *raison d'être* on this earth is summed up in the statement, 'he came to testify to the light' (John 1:8). The apostle Paul says something very similar in Acts 20:24, summing up his own life: 'I do not count my life of any value to myself, if only I may finish my course and the ministry that I received from the Lord Jesus, to testify to the good news of God's grace.'

We live in a culture which prizes 'self-expression' and 'self-realization' – and which makes idols of those who express and realize themselves, whether in business, or sport, or music, or on stage or screen. They 'arrive', somehow, as people, along with the recording contract, the house in the country or their first million. John the Baptist was such a person – mobbed by thousands who travelled for days on foot to hear him speak and be baptized by him. He could have developed a cult following amounting to a mass movement; but he refused. Instead he pointed away from himself to 'the one who is coming after me', whose boot-boy he is not worthy to be (John 1:27). Are we ready to be like that? To give up our autonomy and our desire for self-realization, instead to see ourselves as wholly 'there' for others, for Another, for the Christ who is the Light of the world?

Our Old Testament reading is the famous passage which Jesus applies to himself in his Nazareth sermon (Luke 4:16–19) and which expresses just this sense of being anointed and commissioned to act and speak, not for ourselves, but for the Lord. Many organizations have a 'mission statement', by which their activity is guided and judged. A good exercise, in response to today's readings – and as preparation for Christmas – would be to compose a mission statement for yourself, expressing how Jesus Christ shapes your sense of yourself and your ambitions for the future. 'You are not your own!' Paul tells the Corinthians. 'You were bought with a price!' (1 Corinthians 6:19–20).

★　　★　　★

The Fourth Sunday of Advent

2 Samuel 7:1–11, 16
Luke 1:47–55 *or* Psalm 89:1–4, 19–26
Romans 16:25–27
Luke 1:26–38

P EOPLE are sometimes puzzled by the emphasis placed on Jesus as 'the son of David' in the Christmas story. What does this title signify?

The answer begins in the story in our Old Testament passage. Now firmly established on the throne, David toys with a plan to build a 'house' for God – that is, a Temple in Jerusalem. However, God resists this worthy idea, and turns the tables on David by promising instead to build a 'house' for him – that is, a royal dynasty: 'Your house and your kingdom shall be made sure for ever before me; your throne shall be established for ever' (2 Samuel 7:16). This promise to the 'house' of David became very important in Israel's history, because it seemed to guarantee the future of Jerusalem and the kingdom based there. We see this confidence expressed in today's Psalm.

However, it is worth casting an eye forward to the last part of the same Psalm, verses 35 onwards, where this confidence that 'his line shall continue for ever' (v. 36) is exploded: 'But now you have spurned and rejected him . . . you have renounced the covenant with your servant, you have defiled his crown . . .' (vv. 38–39). This refers to the dreadful events of 587 BCE, when Jerusalem was destroyed by the Babylonians, the Temple razed to the ground, and the King carried off into exile with most of the population. 'Ethnic cleansing' is no modern invention. This created a great crisis of faith, as well as enormous personal suffering for many. How was this compatible with God's promise to the 'house' of David?

Through the centuries which followed, Jews retained their expectation that one day, somehow, the dynasty of David would be

8

restored to the throne in Jerusalem. Some felt that the promise was fulfilled in the second century BCE, when the Maccabean rulers briefly restored Israel's independence; but they were not directly descended from David, and so not all agreed that the promise had been fulfilled. Others felt that the dynasty of Herod, starting in 27 BCE, fitted the bill, particularly because Herod rebuilt the Temple in Jerusalem; but the Herods were Idumeans, not even true Jews, and certainly not descended from David. And so again not all agreed.

In the meantime 'the son of David' became the most common Jewish title for the coming Messiah whom all expected, and there were many like old Simeon who were looking for 'the consolation of Israel' (Luke 2:25). This is the essential background to the angel's announcement to Mary. Luke sets the scene by telling us firmly that she is 'of the house of David' (Luke 1:27). No quibbles here. And the announcement is of one who will sit on 'the throne of his father David' and reign for ever (vv. 32–33). In this coming King, the promise, so long held in abeyance, will at last be fulfilled.

But what sort of a King will he be? And how will he enter his rule? The immediate expectation is – mighty, and by force. Finally all pretenders will be banished, all enemies expelled, all doubts satisfied, and the just and gentle rule prophesied by Isaiah will be secured (Isaiah 9:2–7). That is the expectation, here at the beginning of the story.

Luke looks forward to exploding that plan, as the story unfolds. The promise will be kept, but God has something altogether greater and more wonderful in mind than just another king on David's old throne.

Christmas Eve

2 Samuel 7:1–5, 8–11,16
Psalm 89:2, 21–27
Acts 13:16–26
Luke 1:67–79

AT Christmas the Jewish roots of the Christian faith become clearer than at any other time. In our Gospel we look out through the eyes of Zechariah the priest at what God is doing, and hear him explain it in very Jewish terms. Luke even reflects the distinctive Old Testament terms and phrases which Zechariah would have used – expressions like 'horn of salvation' (v. 69) and 'prophet of the Most High' (v. 76). We must never forget that the Christian Good News came 'to the Jew first, and also to the Greek' (Romans 1:16). Paul was apostle to the Gentiles, but his message in our New Testament reading from Acts is true to his letters: 'My brothers, you descendants of Abraham's family . . . to us the message of this salvation has been sent' (Acts 13:26).

It is deeply right that Zechariah's song, known as the Benedictus, has had such prominent use in Christian liturgy; every time we sing it, we remind ourselves of our Jewish roots. 'Salvation' is the great theme of the song (vv. 69, 71, 77). Zechariah sees this salvation in traditional Jewish terms, and yet at the same time we catch a hint of the new, surprising direction it will take. 'Salvation' means God acting in fulfilment of his promise to David (v. 69) and to Abraham (vv. 72–73), to save Israel from her enemies (vv. 71, 74), so that she might live in peace (v. 79). Zechariah knows that 'holiness and righteousness' (v. 75) cannot be properly achieved before God without political stability and security, because they depend on the settled lifestyle of obedience to the Law, worship in the Temple and community living within the Land God gave.

However, Luke knows differently. By the time we get to the end of his second volume, the Acts of the Apostles, all this has been changed. Now God's people has become worldwide, and includes

Gentiles alongside Jews, the Good News is being preached in Rome, the worship of the Temple has been left behind, and 'holiness and righteousness' are no longer defined by obedience to the Jewish law. Zechariah could never have taken all that on board; but he too points, unwittingly, in this direction when he alludes to Isaiah's prophecy at the end of his song: '. . . to give light to those who sit in darkness and in the shadow of death . . .' (v. 79). This comes from Isaiah 9:2, the famous passage where Isaiah prophesies 'a great light' for 'the people who walked in darkness': 'those who lived in a land of deep darkness, on them light has shined'. Israel walked in darkness at various points in her history, but supremely those who 'live in darkness' are not the Jews at all, but all the Gentile nations who had no special covenant relationship with the God of Abraham. Isaiah knew this, and makes it clear that he has 'Galilee of the Gentiles' in mind. Simeon picks up the same theme: this baby, he says, is 'a light for revelation to the Gentiles' (Luke 2:32).

Luke loves this thought! The old mould is broken, the excluded Gentiles are brought in, and 'the forgiveness of sins' is offered to all who need it (v. 77), not just to the descendants of Abraham. That's the Christmas message!

★　★　★

Christmas Day
First set of readings

Isaiah 9:2–7
Psalm 96
Titus 2:11–14
Luke 2:1–14 *or* 1–20

ISAIAH 9:2–7 is one of the most famous Old Testament Christmas readings. It is important to notice its passionate anti-war emphasis. The gift of this child, the coming King on David's throne who will rule for ever with justice and righteousness, will mean a final end to war and oppression, 'as on the day of Midian' – reminding

11

us of the story in Judges 6–7 about Gideon's victory over the Midianites with 300 men armed only with clay pots and torches. 'The myth of redemptive violence' – an expression coined by Professor Walter Wink of Union Seminary, New York – is one of the most powerful in western culture. From children playing 'goodies' and 'baddies', through countless westerns, thrillers, cartoons and Superman movies, to the use of bombers in Iraq and Kosovo, we have accustomed ourselves to believe that force is redemptive, provided it is used by good people for good ends. 'The myth of redemptive violence' conditions people's agonized question, 'Why doesn't God intervene? Why doesn't he step in to stop the bombers and the rapists?' Like Superman from the sky, we want force to be exercised by God – to compel justice and peace.

But he doesn't; because his answer is the gift of a child, not an army. The army is there, of course – and appears sometimes. The heavenly 'host' is actually an angelic army, and occasionally, in the Bible, they produce an overpowering punch-up on earth. They fight alongside Barak (Judges 5:20), David (2 Samuel 5:24) and Jehoshaphat (2 Chronicles 20); and against Pharaoh (Exodus 14:19–25) and the Assyrians (2 Kings 19:35). Jesus, however, didn't want them. He could have called upon twelve legions of them, he said, to rescue him from his enemies, but he did not, for 'all who take the sword will perish by the sword' (Matthew 26:52–53). He knew that redemption comes, not through any myth of violence, but through the cross.

So it is almost as though the heavenly army was resigning that night when, with swords well sheathed, they were recruited into a choir and told to sing about the Saviour born in the city of David. One word from God, and the swords would have been out, and they would have come flashing down, destroying the murderous power of Rome, disabling the armies of oppression and consigning all tyrants to Tartarus. Supermen to the rescue! But that is not God's way. He sends his Son, as a baby, and tells his soldiers to sing. For he wants to win his enemies, not destroy them. 'The grace of God has appeared, bringing salvation to all!' Paul writes in our New Testament reading (Titus 2:11). One day there will be judgment, when the angels will collect all causes of sin and evildoers out of God's Kingdom, and cast them into the furnace (the words of Jesus, Matthew 13:41–42), but in the meantime those angels are kept in their barracks, having singing lessons, while God sends his Son and appeals to the world in his 'grace'.

How does the message get out? Quietly, and one-to-one, as like the shepherds we tell the people we meet the wonderful things that we have heard about this Saviour.

★ ★ ★

Christmas Day
Second set of readings

Isaiah 62:6–12
Psalm 97
Titus 3:4–7
Luke 2:8–20 *or* 1–20

THIS set of readings gives our Christmas celebration a 'mission' feel. It reminds us that the birth of Jesus is not an end, but a beginning – the beginning of a story still being written, in which we all have bit-parts to play.

What changed, that night in Bethlehem? In one sense, the world can never be the same again. God has assumed human flesh, and lives on the surface of our globe. But from another perspective, nothing has changed. For 99% of the inhabitants of Bethlehem, that night was as all others. The shepherds went back to their flocks. That night was succeeded by the next day. The Romans went on ruling. Mary and Joseph started practising the long art of parentcraft.

A long-standing objection to the Christian faith has been that we believe the kingdom came with Jesus, but the world remains unredeemed. How can this be? The answer, of course, is that the story only begins with the coming of Jesus. He starts the process whereby one day the kingdom of God will fill the earth. Our

Old Testament reading pictures watchmen posted on the walls of Jerusalem. But rather than just look for approaching enemies, they lift their sights higher and look for their ultimate hope of security, which rests with the Lord and his promise.

So the watchmen are always talking – not keeping silent until an enemy hoves into view, but speaking out to the Lord. 'You who remind the Lord, take no rest, and give him no rest until he establishes Jerusalem and makes it renowned throughout the earth!' (Isaiah 62:6–7). The watchmen remind themselves that the Lord has sworn to do this (vv. 8–9), and then they call on the rest of the people to go out and prepare the approach-road to the city, so that the Lord their Saviour may enter (vv. 10–12).

Similarly Paul, in our New Testament reading, reminds us that the 'appearance' of God our Saviour does not just mean that we have been saved, but that we become 'heirs according to the hope of eternal life' (Titus 3:7). We have been renewed by the Holy Spirit (v. 5), but this renewal means having a vivid hope of eternal life yet to be. Luke tells this world-changing story in chapter 2 of his 52-chapter, two-volume work. This is just the beginning. He traces the progress of the angels' message through many ups and downs until it reaches the centre of the Empire, the very place where once an idea formed in an Emperor's mind (Luke 2:1) that launched a young couple, over a thousand miles away, on to a hazardous journey with the wife in the last stages of pregnancy, seventy-five arduous miles south from Nazareth to Bethlehem to be registered for tax.

The Emperor was thinking of money, and power, and extending his Empire. But the message that came bouncing back from that obscure corner of his realm, carried to Rome by a prisoner awaiting his judgment, was of the kingdom of God established by the Lord Jesus Christ (Acts 28:31). And the story goes on. That's our task too: to give the Lord no rest as we cry to him to establish his kingdom on earth, the kingdom that began that night but is rejected still, the kingdom of his Christ.

★　　★　　★

Christmas Day
Third set of readings

Isaiah 52:7–10
Psalm 98
Hebrews 1:1–4 *or* 1–12
John 1:1–14

T HIS set of readings is united around the theme of the coming of God. The Isaiah passage pictures a messenger approaching Jerusalem with good news, and then the watchmen on the walls 'in plain sight . . . see the return of the Lord to Zion' (Isaiah 52:8). Alongside this passage the Psalm (familiar to Evensong devotees as the Cantate Domino) bids the whole world rejoice 'at the presence of the Lord, for he is coming to judge the earth' (Psalm 98:9). The beautiful passage from Hebrews calls on all God's angels to worship the Son when he comes as 'the firstborn' into the world (Hebrews 1:6). And our Gospel reading speaks so powerfully of the coming of the light into the world: 'He came to his own home, but his own people did not receive him. But to all who received him, who believed in his name, he gave power to become children of God . . .' (John 1:11–12).

In what sense does God 'come' into his world? At Christmas we remember his coming as an historical event, 2,000 years ago in Bethlehem, but our faith will be meagre and antiquarian if it just commemorates the past. These readings connect that once-for-all coming in the flesh with other sorts of 'coming' to which Christmas points. The tradition of the coming of the Lord to Zion (Isaiah 52) was strong in the first century. It lies behind John the Baptist's preaching ('Prepare the way of the Lord!') and was at the heart of Jewish expectation. It meant that one day God himself would reside in Jerusalem, make it truly the centre of the world, reign from there in peace, bring the nations into submission to himself and to Israel, and usher in a Golden Age.

John is drawing on this tradition when he writes of the light 'coming to his own home' (John 1:11) – although with the sting

15

in the tail, that he was rejected when he arrived. In the New Testament this expectation of God's coming to bring final salvation to his people is applied also to the second coming of Christ.

Then there is the coming in universal judgment, celebrated in today's Psalm. 'He comes to judge the earth' means that he issues the decrees which will finally sort right from wrong, and create justice for all, punishing the wicked and saving the righteous. This is what John the Baptist expected Jesus to do, according to Matthew 3:12. But he was puzzled when Jesus failed to do it (Matthew 11:2–3). Jesus did not see his mission in those terms. 'I did not come to judge the world, but to save it (John 12:47). The coming in judgment is pushed out into the future.

Thirdly there is the coming in glory, celebrated in our Hebrews reading. We can link this with many passages which associate God's glory with the glorification of Jesus, and look forward to a final moment or 'day' when Jesus's true position and nature will no longer be veiled, but fully and finally recognized.

Lastly there is the coming to those who believe, which John emphasizes in our Gospel (1:12). This we celebrate not just at Christmas, but with every act of worship, with every moment of prayer, and with every venture of faith by which we seek to 'receive' him now and admit him into partnership in our everyday lives. Thus we too become 'children of God'!

★   ★   ★

The First Sunday of Christmas

Isaiah 61:10–62:3
Psalm 148
Galatians 4:4–7
Luke 2:15–21

'So they went with haste, and found Mary and Joseph, and the child lying in the manger' (Luke 2:16); it was all so ordinary.

But behind the ordinariness, what depths of magic and marvel! There was nothing particularly odd about a baby in a manger; the 'manger' was the trough in which hay to feed the animals was placed, in the large living-space shared by animals and humans together in a typical first-century Judean dwelling. Usually, the human family would occupy a raised platform filling one half, and the manger would stand against this platform. So, if nothing else was available for a new-born baby because the house was bursting at the seams with visitors, he might well be laid in the manger. Not very odd, but sufficiently odd to distinguish Jesus from any other babies born that night.

The shepherds knew they had found the right place; it looked so ordinary. But out on the hills the shepherds had heard an extraordinary tale, of a Saviour-Messiah born that night in Bethlehem, and they had seen the heavenly army-turned-choir singing glory to God and peace on earth. Then they rubbed their eyes, and the sight was gone, and there was just a baby in a manger.

'Heaven in ordinary' said George Herbert, describing prayer. The shepherds would have known what he meant. Why did the army not sing above the town? Why only out on the hills? Because this Saviour comes not with huge fanfares, but with the excited, stumbling testimony of a group of ordinary shepherds. Yes, so run-of-the-mill; a mother, a father and a baby. What could look more ordinary than that?

But Joseph and Mary know the hidden story. They know that Joseph had no part in this birth. Reflecting on this, Paul emphasizes the action of God, who 'when the fullness of time had come, sent his Son, born of a woman, born under the law, to redeem those under the law, that we might receive adoption as children' (Galatians 4:4–5). Theologians speculate about the reason for the 'Virgin Birth', and wonder whether it has something to do with freeing Jesus from the taint of Original Sin. But the New Testament knows nothing of such a reason. Wherever the Virgin Birth is mentioned in the New Testament (Matthew 1:18–25, Luke 1:30–38, Galatians 4:4) it is clear that its purpose is to preserve God's initiative and to underline Jesus's intimate relation to him. He is God's Son, born at the time determined by God and by no other, 'sent' to fulfil the plan God has actioned, and uniquely equipped by the Spirit for the task.

But for all that, he is just a baby, lying in a manger, completely dependent upon his parents like all new-borns, rubbed with salt and tied with strips of cloth to straighten his little limbs. Mary and Joseph feel nervous like all new parents. They also know that their all-too-ordinary inexperience puts at risk more than one tiny life. Heaven holds its breath to see how they will manage.

For us, too, heaven lies in the ordinary. Our stumbling words too may testify to the wonderful reality of this Christ-child who shares our world, our sin and our death, and brings heaven to birth in the manger of our hearts.

★   ★   ★

Second Sunday of Christmas

Jeremiah 31:7–14 *or* Sirach 24:1–12
Psalm 147:12–20 *or* Wisdom of Solomon 10:15–21
Ephesians 1:3–14
John 1:10–18 *or* John 1:1–18

I T is probably a good idea to choose the alternative set of readings today, so as to read Ecclesiasticus 24 alongside John 1. This chapter of Ecclesiasticus (or 'Sirach') is one of the most important pieces of background to the presentation of Jesus as the 'Word' of God in John's Prologue. The 'wisdom' tradition, exemplified in Sirach 24, was Israel's way of coping with the 'problem of transcendence'. This is a problem that faces all theistic belief-systems, that is, religions or philosophies that assert the existence of a supreme deity.

The question is, does this deity act within the world, and if so, how? This question was felt particularly sharply in the ancient world, because the Greek philosophical tradition tended to regard the matter of the world around us as either intrinsically evil or at the least incompatible with the divine. How, then, can there be any contact between God and the world? The doctrine of creation helps the Old Testament to overcome the 'problem of transcendence', for if God was involved with the world when making it, then presumably he can continue to act within it. But then the little difficulty of sin rears its ugly head. How can God in his absolute holiness remain in contact with a sinful world? The tabernacle, pointedly known as the 'tent of meeting' (e.g. Exodus 33:7), shows the answer of the Old Testament: God takes up residence in the middle of his chosen people, but they can only actually 'meet' him through an elaborate system of sacrifices, and even then he remains in splendid isolation in the 'Most Holy Place' at the centre of the tabernacle.

In any case, how real is this thought of God 'dwelling' in a tent or building? Dedicating the Temple, Solomon hits the nail on the head. God is supposed to inhabit the Temple, but 'will God indeed dwell on the earth? Even heaven and the highest heaven cannot contain you, much less this house that I have built!' (1 Kings 8:27).

This is where 'the wisdom of God' comes in. If God himself remains aloof, his wisdom need not. In Sirach 24 God's 'wisdom' is pictured as acting independently of God himself, 'coming forth' from God (v. 3), 'seeking' a resting-place on earth (v. 7), then 'commanded' by God to 'make your dwelling in Jacob' (v. 3), particularly in the Temple in Jerusalem (vv. 10–11). Later in the chapter, this 'wisdom' of God is identified with the book of the law of God, Israel's most prized expression of God's presence in her midst (Sirach 24:23). 'Make your dwelling in Jacob', says Sirach 24:8, and here the same unusual Greek word is used as in John 1:14, 'the Word became flesh and dwelt among us'.

Like wisdom, God's word comes from him, and seeks a dwelling, coming to 'his own' (v. 11), but finding a resting-place not in Israel generally but among all 'those who believed in his name' (v. 12). In the most dramatic way possible, the problem of transcendence is tackled by asserting the incarnation of the wisdom of God. God is present now, not through some vague quality ('wisdom') expressed in a book, but in a person of flesh and blood who is his 'Word', that is, his very mind and heart expressed into

19

human form and speech, and living 'among us' so that we can 'behold his glory' (v. 14). What a message!

★   ★   ★

The Epiphany

Isaiah 60:1–6
Psalm 72:10–15 *or* 1–15
Ephesians 3:1–12
Matthew 2:1–12

THOUGH in many ways the most Jewish of the four Gospels, Matthew nonetheless has a special interest in Jesus's relevance for the whole world. He uniquely concludes his Gospel with the Great Commission (Matthew 28:18–20) and foreshadows this universal proclamation at several points within his story of Jesus: in the parable of the Sheep and the Goats (25:31–46), the universal coming of the Son of Man (24:30–31), the stories of the Syro-Phoenician woman (15:21–28) and the believing centurion (8:5–13), the long quotation from Isaiah 42 in 12:18–21, with the addition of the phrase 'in his name the Gentiles will hope', the mission of the twelve in 10:16–18 – and of course through this famous story of the Magi.

Matthew has already prepared the way for it by including Rahab the Canaanite prostitute and Ruth the Moabitess in his royal genealogy of Jesus (Matthew 1:5). These two women, from outside Israel but essential to the royal line, point forward to the Magi who are the first to recognize and worship the Christ. In fact Matthew paints a horrible contrast between Herod and the Magi. They are guided only by the uncertain voice of a star, yet they travel miles to offer costly gifts and worship to 'the King of the Jews'. Herod the Jew, on the other hand, is guided by the certain voice of prophecy (Micah 5:2–4, verse 6), but he does not budge from Jerusalem, and his intentions towards the new-born king are far from worshipful. This contrast points forward to Jesus's words about the centurion, 'Many will come from east and west and will eat with Abraham and Isaac and Jacob in the kingdom of heaven, while the heirs of the kingdom will be thrown into the outer darkness' (Matthew 8:11–12).

The Magi remind us of the sheer, exuberant variety of the kingdom of God. We can see it all today in the world-wide church of Jesus Christ: such a multiplicity of cultures, colours, languages, styles, even theologies. Imagine a flying tour: starting in a formal, restrained word-centred Reformed church somewhere in northern Europe you fly to St Peter's, Rome, where music and symbolic action speak vastly and magnificently; thence to a small Orthodox church in Greece, where icons, dark colour and sonorous singing underline the distinction between heaven and earth; now you're off to a Gospel choir in Harlem, New York, where poverty has given birth to deep and enthusiastic faith within the black community; now to a huge, prosperous Baptist church in Atlanta, Georgia, with a vast programme of social welfare and missionary work; and finally to a youth church somewhere in urban Britain, where worshippers don't just sing the hymns but dance to them. Can this all be the same church?

Matthew would have no doubts. He loves the picture of these strange astrologers suddenly appearing in Jerusalem, come to worship the Christ. He does not endorse astrology, of course, for his point is that they now worship Christ, not the astral powers. But they illustrate the wonderful variety of the many who stream into the kingdom from east and west: something to celebrate today!

★   ★   ★

The Baptism of Christ

(The First Sunday of Epiphany)

Genesis 1:1–5
Psalm 29
Acts 19:1–7
Mark 1:4–11

EPIPHANY explores the mystery of the incarnation, and the revelation of Jesus to the world. This Sunday dedicated to his baptism gets us going well, for the story of Jesus's baptism forms a nice 'pair' with that of the Magi. At the beginning of his life, the Magi symbolize his revelation to the world, a sign of his universal meaning; at the beginning of his ministry, his baptism marks his revelation to Israel, a sign of his meaning for his people. The story of the Magi involves the heavenly sign of the star; his baptism involves the voice from heaven and the descending dove. Both stories involve a confession: the Magi call him 'the king of Israel', but in the baptism the heavenly voice calls him 'my Son'.

But there are differences also: most notably, that the story of the Magi only appears in Matthew's Gospel, whereas all four Gospels begin their accounts of Jesus's public ministry with the story of his baptism. Clearly they all thought it most important; so what does it teach? We restrict ourselves to Mark's account, read today. Firstly, Jesus associates himself with Israel's renewal through John the Baptist. John created a great stir (v. 5), and what would today be called a 'revival'; great moral seriousness gripped people, and a deep sense of repentance. By his dress John associated himself with Elijah (v. 6, cf. 2 Kings 1:8), who likewise had called Israel back to God after a period of loss of faith. In the middle of that huge crowd Jesus comes for baptism, associating himself with the longing for renewal that he sees all around him. He will have a great hand in making it fruitful.

But he is different from all those around him, for, secondly, Jesus does not make a confession, but receives one. Everyone else was confessing sins, but Jesus heard God's confession of his true identity as his Son, and God's verdict on him (v. 11). God is pleased with him, he has no sins to mar his relationship with God. Mark presents the dove and the voice as a private revelation to Jesus. He alone is aware of this 'rending' of heaven.

But at the other end of the story there is a matching confession and 'rending' which is thoroughly public. As Jesus breathes his last upon the cross, the centurion confesses 'Truly this man was God's Son!', and at that moment something else is 'rent' – not heaven, but something with similar import: the curtain of the Temple, standing before the Most Holy Place, symbolizing the division between God and the world (Mark 14:38–39). Now access to God is open, and free, for sin no longer creates an insuperable barrier.

And what's more, thirdly, Jesus prepares the way for 'the baptism of the Holy Spirit'. The descending dove picks up John's prophecy that he will baptize with the Spirit. In a unique way, Jesus is not just empowered by the Spirit, but empowered to bestow the Spirit. This never happens within Mark's Gospel itself. Mark leaves us, like the disciples of John the Baptist in Acts 19:1–7, to discover what it means to go beyond just repentance and confession of sin, into the deeply renewed life that Christ alone can give, through the Spirit.

★　　★　　★

The Second Sunday of Epiphany

1 Samuel 3:1–10 *or* 1–20
Psalm 139:1–6, 13–18
Revelation 5:1–10
John 1:43–51

THE revelation of Jesus to Israel at his baptism has to be matched and completed by a 'revealing' of himself to individual people. In fact, this is the most important sort of 'revelation'. Jesus was actually hidden in the crowd around John the Baptist; the dove and the voice were private experiences given to him alone.

For us, too, Jesus has no significance unless he is 'revealed' to us, as he was to Philip and Nathanael in our Gospel passage. Otherwise, he is just hidden in the crowd of people who clamour around us, seeking our allegiance. What distinguishes Jesus from the Buddha, from Mohammed, from Marx and Freud and the Maharishi and all the gurus of our post-modern, hedonistic culture? What makes his voice different? The answer is that, as the apostle Paul puts it, Jesus alone 'calls' with the voice of God himself (see for instance Romans 1:6–7, 9:24; 1 Corinthians 7:18–24; 2 Thessalonians 2:14).

For Paul this 'calling' is a spiritual experience, a revelation when faith is born and the Spirit is given. 'Faith arises out of hearing, and true hearing from the word spoken by Christ himself,' he writes (Romans 10:17). With most of us it will not be a physical hearing of God's voice, as with Samuel in our Old Testament reading, nor an apocalyptic vision as in Revelation 5; but it may be just as difficult to discern whether we are really hearing the voice of God. Samuel thought it was the voice of his mentor Eli, and similarly we can often confuse God's voice with the various drives and impulses coming to us from our background. Wish-fulfilment and guilt can masquerade as the voice of God. Similarly we can be uncertain as to what exactly God is saying, like Philip and Nathanael.

What led Philip to conclude that Jesus was the prophet promised by Moses (John 1:45 – cf. Deuteronomy 18:15)? Later, John's Gospel makes it clear that Jesus is much greater than this. Nathanael grasps after something greater with his confession of Jesus as 'the Son of God, the King of Israel' (1:49).

Does he know what he means by these terms? Philip and Nathanael were gripped and fascinated by Jesus, and struggled for words to express why they felt inclined to 'follow' him, to respond to his call (1:43). This is at the heart of all true faith. In the midst of our confusion and uncertainty there grows the conviction of something solid, lasting and deeply true in the person of Jesus – and a conviction that he is not just a figure of the past, but alive to be encountered today. This is the conviction expressed in our Psalm. The Psalmist knows the reality of God in his life, and rejoices to be made, and known, and protected by God. It is the 'call' that produces such conviction.

We too can experience that 'Follow me!' addressed to us by the Spirit of Christ; and almost always such a 'call' will come as a result of getting to know him, like Philip and Nathanael: reading the Gospels, discussing the faith with others, weighing the evidence, trying it out. Sometimes the 'call' will come at a specific moment, but often the awareness of it grows slowly over a period of time. Epiphany invites us into a living experience of Christ for ourselves.

★   ★   ★

The Third Sunday of Epiphany

Genesis 14:17–20
Psalm 128
Revelation 19:6–10
John 2:1–11

THESE readings follow neatly from last Sunday's set and develop further the theme of the creation of faith. It is fascinating to reflect on the fact that faith can be either strengthened or undermined by precisely the same experiences. For instance, bereavement or illness will drive person A away from Christ and the church, because of the insistent question 'Why?' or 'Why me?' which never receives an answer. Person B, however, will be prompted into a much closer relationship with Christ through the same experience. What makes the difference? These readings illustrate four ways in which faith is created and sustained, and point to the factors which give experiences a positive, rather than negative, effect.

Our Psalm illustrates the settled, prosperous lifestyle which some enjoy. For some people, life seems to offer no upsets! Their work generates plenty of money, their children are healthy and well-adjusted, and they remain physically fit into a prosperous old age. Such well-being could make people careless about God, but the Psalm celebrates those who are filled with thankfulness towards him, who see their possessions as blessings, and who 'fear the Lord' as a result – that is, they serve him with deep reverence.

Abraham in Genesis 14 illustrates those for whom a significant encounter is a vital catalyst. Abraham recognizes Melchizedek as a 'priest of God Most High', and gives him a tithe of the spoils he has just won in battle. Most Christians have experienced an encounter with someone so obviously saintly that they feel inspired to greater love and self-sacrifice. For some, such a contact can be deeply life-changing, introducing a whole new experience of God himself. In Revelation 19 we meet a group of suffering people who have been through social isolation, probably also persecution, for their faith. What has sustained them is worship, arising from their vision of God and of Christ. They know that 'our God the Almighty reigns', and that they have been invited into intimate fellowship with Christ, pictured as a marriage-feast. So they 'hold the testimony of Jesus' (19:10), despite the consequences.

Finally our Gospel reading takes us to the root of it all by presenting the manifestation of the glory of Christ as the vital factor. The disciples see his glory revealed in the 'sign' of the water-into-wine, and 'believe in him'. They illustrate the way in which experiences of all sorts may lead us to a deeper understanding of Christ himself. Though the disciples must have been puzzled about the exact import of this strange happening, their view of Jesus was changed for ever. What unites all these diverse experiences is a self-forgetful focus upon God, and upon Christ, and a response of worship and faith towards the God revealed.

This sounds as though it just gives a circular answer to the question with which we began: experiences have a positive effect on faith for those who respond with positive faith! But we can say more than this. For suffering or prosperity sap faith when people turn inward upon themselves, lose the vision of a Christ who really exists above and beyond them, and to whom they owe a response of love and worship in and through all the varied circumstances of life. Those who add 'For you, Jesus!' to all life's challenges truly find that (as George Herbert puts it) 'This is the famous stone, that turneth all to gold'.

★   ★   ★

The Fourth Sunday of Epiphany

Deuteronomy 18:15–20
Psalm 111
Revelation 12:1–5a
Mark 1:21–28

I T would be possible to be very jealous of John the prophet, the author of the book of Revelation. Surely it was no longer possible for him to doubt the reality of Christ, having received such an amazing series of visions, like the one we read today. If only we had such experiences! But if I had a dream like this vision, I would wake wondering whether it was a product of feverish imagination, or a gift from God. I would still need to ask, how is true revelation recognized as such, and distinguished from the counterfeit?

This question is highly appropriate for Epiphany. We find it tackled within the Bible, and not least by our Old Testament and Gospel readings today. Deuteronomy 18:15–20 contains the Lord's promise to raise up another prophet like Moses, whom the people are commanded to heed. The passage naturally anticipates the question, 'How will we recognize this prophet when the time comes?', and offers two tests of the true prophet.

The first test is doctrinal and social (v. 20): any prophecy offered in the name of another god, effectively outside the community of Israel, is not authentic. The second is practical (vv. 21–22 – it would be good to include these in the reading): if the prophecy does not come to pass, it is clearly false. It is not hard to apply these two tests today, and indeed we can see them being applied to Jesus in our Gospel reading. Jesus passes the doctrinal and social test, because he delivers his 'new teaching' not in the name of a new god, but in the setting of ordinary synagogue worship, dedicated to the worship of the God of Israel. People expected prophecy to be new, and authoritative, unlike the teaching of the scribes (v. 22) which focused on reporting and debating the opinions of other scribes. Jesus fitted the bill – new, authoritative teaching but within the setting and structures of first-century Judaism.

This forms a solid test for us too. Authentic experience of God, which we might call personal revelation of him, is always to be found within the boundaries of the church of Jesus Christ, and in continuity with the traditions of the church. It will not necessarily be bound by those traditions, and indeed church history tells the story of many powerful 'movements' of the Spirit of God which have upset current traditions and created something dramatically new – as Jesus did, within first-century Judaism. But there will always be a deep sense of social and doctrinal continuity with what has gone before.

Jesus passes the second, practical test with flying colours also, as the 'unclean spirit' is overpowered and this poor man released. Jesus's prophetic word, 'Be silent! And come out of him!' (v. 25), is amply vindicated by its effect. We too may judge the authenticity of any claimed experiences of God – including our own! – by this test of fruitfulness: is there truly a sense of the forgiveness of sin, is there new joy and love, does reconciliation result, are old hurts and wounds dealt with and healed, does worship become a delight?

Questions like these will test and reveal the genuineness of our experience of God.

★   ★   ★

The Presentation of Christ in the Temple
(Candlemas)

Malachi 3:1–5
Psalm 24:1–6 *or* 1–10
Hebrews 2:14–18
Luke 2:22–40

O UR Psalm and Old Testament reading set the scene by pointing to the coming of the Lord to Zion as background to the Gospel story of the presentation of the infant Jesus in the Temple in Jerusalem. (See the comments above on the third set of readings for Christmas Day, which explore this tradition a little.)

Luke makes Jesus's appearance in the Temple so significant, greeted with profound words of prophecy, that we can well believe this tradition is in his mind. At last the promise has been fulfilled, and the Lord's Christ has appeared in the Temple, the 'messenger of the covenant' (Malachi 3:1) who brings cleansing to Israel and light to the Gentiles! Luke's introduction to the story in 2:22–24 is a masterpiece of subtle allusion to three Old Testament themes, which underline the reality and purpose of the incarnation most movingly.

Firstly, he tells us that the visit took place because 'the days of their purification were complete' (v. 22). This refers to the regulations in Leviticus 12:1–8. The process of childbirth was held to make women ritually impure for forty days. At the end of this period mothers had to present themselves at the Temple, to offer the sacrifice noted by Luke here (v. 24) – which, incidentally, was the sacrifice prescribed for poor families. The reality of Jesus's humanity is powerfully pictured here: his birth makes his mother unclean, like the birth of any other child. As the author of Hebrews puts it, 'since the children share flesh and blood, he himself likewise shared the same things' (Hebrews 2:14). He steps into the muddy waters of our physicality, with all its capacity to stain and smear, so that we might be saved.

Secondly, Luke mentions that Joseph and Mary were also concerned with the regulations concerning the firstborn male. In Exodus 13:2, which Luke quotes in verse 23, God claims all firstborn males for himself. The firstborn of every cow, sheep or goat had to be sacrificed, symbolizing God's possession (Numbers 18:17), but firstborn human beings had to be 'redeemed' with a money-offering (Numbers 18:15–16, also Exodus 13:12–13). Luke is reminding us of the words of the angel to Mary in 1.35, 'The Holy Spirit shall come upon you . . . therefore what is born shall be called holy, the son of God'. In Jesus's case, this old law takes on a new meaning. He belongs to his Father in a unique, special sense, but also in the same way as all first-born Jews.

Joseph and Mary did not need actually to bring the baby to the Temple for either of these two reasons, Mary's purification and the offering of the redemption-price. However, Luke emphasizes that they came 'to present him to the Lord' (v. 22). What were they doing? There is no mention of a money-offering, as required for the redemption, and so we are reminded, thirdly, of another sort of offering – like that of Samuel, given by his mother Hannah for the service of the Lord in his Temple (1 Samuel 1:1–2:11). No redemption-price was needed, for, like Samuel, this firstborn was actually given to the Lord, presented to him in his Temple to be 'holy' to him.

The Presentation of Christ thus speaks both of his deep association with us, in our fallen humanity, and of his dedication to a unique service of God on our behalf.

★ ★ ★

Ordinary Time – Proper 1

(Sunday between 3 and 9 February – the Fifth Sunday after Epiphany)

Isaiah 40:21–31
Psalm 147:1–11, 20c
1 Corinthians 9:16–23
Mark 1:29–39

T HE Epiphany season is over: Christmas and the revelation of Jesus's identity give way to a short season of 'ordinary time' before Lent and Holy Week demand our attention. As the rich imagery of Epiphany recedes and the rigours of Lent still stretch ahead, the lectionary gives us a moment to stand on one side, acknowledging nostalgia for the past and our hunger for a different future, a moment to turn round and, from today's readings, to acknowledge dependence on God both for our commission and for its empowering.

The Old Testament reading addresses the inevitable question of a situation of defeat and exile, 'Does our God still want to have anything to do with us?' The prophet revives the praise of the people. God is extolled for the majesty of his creation, but this is just the sign of his great goodness as Lord of history. In a direct challenge to the astral gods of Babylon, he is the one who calls the stars by name. 'He gives power to the faint, and strengthens the powerless.' The Psalm too describes the intimate security which God's care gives – the rejection of a false self-confidence that relies on human skill alone.

Paul is entrusted with a commission to proclaim the gospel, he bears the office of 'slave of Christ', an expression borrowed from the imperial household. He insists that he possesses as much apostolic authority as anyone, and he is confident of the love of God. The Christians at Corinth liked the idea of their 'spiritual liberty', which they understood as essential to the gospel, but Paul imposes a serious limitation on this for the sake of the 'weaker brethren'. They thought their salvation was assured, but Paul does not share this kind of assurance. The new relation to God which he has in Christ expresses rather a debt of obedience.

As we move into 'ordinary time', we embark on a continuous reading from Mark's Gospel. The early verses have been used in Advent and Epiphany; the stories of John the Baptist and of the calling of the disciples lie in the background. Here we encounter Mark's conviction that healing is a sign of God's coming rule. As the Gospel begins we have encountered the negative destruction of an 'evil spirit' which has to be driven out. The healing of Peter's mother-in-law expresses a more positive aspect – she can serve their sabbath meal! But it remains a sign: the exercise of this extraordinary power is not to be confined to what we call 'miracles', and we do well not to be distracted by them. The 'whole town' may gather, but Jesus renews his strength in a solitary place and insists that he must keep moving on. He leaves Capernaum at the height of his popularity, everyone seeking him out yet unable to nail his true identity and its implications – unlike the demons.

Mark's firm conviction is that God will make well all that is not well. The demons know who Jesus is – but that is all they know! Ambiguity is emphasized by Jesus's decision to leave Capernaum at the height of his popularity, when everyone is seeking him out for the wrong reason.

★   ★   ★

Proper 2
(Sunday between 10 and 16 February – the Sixth Sunday after Epiphany)

2 Kings 5:1–14
Psalm 30
1 Corinthians 9:24–27
Mark 1:40–45

TODAY's readings provide us with a moment to check the compass and admire the view, to be realistic about freedom and its demands.

First the healing of Naaman. This is one of a small number of treasured passages which shows Israel's God caring for people of all races; for everyone is made in God's image. The theology is similar to that of Second Isaiah and the story of Jonah: not 'universalism' exactly, but a sense of privilege which makes Israel 'light to the nations' and calls her to awesome global responsibilities.

Psalm 30 was, according to its superscription, used at the Feast of Dedication to commemorate the restoration of Temple worship after its desecration by Antiochus Epiphanes: a reinterpretation of the experiences of an individual as referring to those of the community. Through sickness the poet comes to realize that he has built the security of his life on a false foundation. The conquering of his self-centredness becomes, therefore, a sign for the whole community of the grace of God on which they are to rely.

The New Testament readings continue from last week. Paul pursues his debate with the Corinthians, maintaining that Christianity involves the limitation as well as the enjoyment of freedom. His own willing surrender of privilege for the sake of the gospel is one form of such discipline. Using athletic metaphors, perhaps from the Isthmian games established in Corinth, he encourages the Christian community not to imagine that they have already 'arrived', but to commit themselves to the race.

The healing of the leper, echoing the Naaman story, shows powers which go further than anything up to this point in the Gospel. Leprosy, as well as being 'unclean', was believed to be incurable. The language is very strong, and Mark seems to understand Jesus's anger and emotion as caused by the forces of evil with which he is in conflict. Clearly he wanted the healing to carry with it a spiritual obligation. There is some suggestion that he feared being hindered by crowds looking for physical miracles only. Again the point is made: outward healing is a sign of more profound changes afoot. Privilege and freedom carry the responsibility of obedience and self-discipline.

★   ★   ★

Proper 3
(Sunday between 17 and 23 February – the Seventh after Epiphany)

Isaiah 43:18–25
Psalm 41
2 Corinthians 1:18–22
Mark 2:1–12

THE continuities of the Corinthian correspondence and of readings from Mark's Gospel break off after this Sunday – and are not resumed until after Trinity. For today, the sense of taking bearings and checking the direction is pursued a bit further. The proclamation of forgiveness seems to round off the three Sundays concerned with dependence on God and with freedom and responsibility.

The Old Testament reading calls the people of Israel to stop looking back mournfully and clinging nostalgically to the past. A new, miraculous act of God lies ahead. At its centre lies the proclamation of forgiveness (v. 25). The new deliverance will become reality by a new journey through the transformed wilderness. This new Exodus will echo in the praises of the people – and the echo will reverberate out, way beyond their immediate circle.

The Psalm is a prayer for wholeness – an act of faith – asking for forgiveness and lamenting the betrayal of friends.

2 Corinthians is less well-ordered than 1 Corinthians, possibly an amalgam of letters originally distinct. In this passage Paul is arguing for his dependability in reply to some in Corinth who think him unreliable for changing a planned visit to them. He is maintaining that his travels in the service of the Gospel are governed by a

profound vision of his mission and message. There is a play on the word 'anointed' which our translations of verse 22 miss: God 'christed' Paul, marking him with a seal as belonging to Christ, and gifting him with the Spirit. God has made Paul another Christ, which means that he gives him the grace to be as totally reliable as Christ was.

The Gospel story both builds on an old theme, 'Who is this man?', and introduces a new one, 'Who can forgive sins but God alone?', and this begins a conflict with the Jewish leaders which will lead ultimately to Jesus's rejection and death. The paralytic, like the leper, is shut off from life. Jesus deals with the root problem: for Mark, healing and forgiveness belong together – Jesus is accused of claiming to do what only God can do. The scribes are incensed with good reason. Only they, as interpreters of God's law, think they have any 'authority on earth'. The Son of Man (a title which carries ideas of suffering and final vindication) is wresting this away from them by identifying with the crowd; a warning to all religious people who think they can claim special privileges.

★   ★   ★

The Second Sunday before Lent

Proverbs 8:1, 22–31
Psalm 104:24–35
Colossians 1:15–20
John 1:1–14

THE reading of the Prologue to John's Gospel marks the turning towards Lent and Holy Week. No longer simply the Christmas message of incarnation, here rejection is anticipated even as the goodness and glory of creation is celebrated. It is the latter which is in focus – a reminder of significance and identity before the build-up of our protective disguise is stripped away.

The Old Testament reading from Proverbs constitutes a poem about Wisdom's part in creation. She repeatedly describes her divine authority before anything was created. More important, she is all delight, rejoicing before God and delighting in his human creatures. This is very different from the creation account of Genesis 1 and of the Canaanite conception of the world emerging from the conflict between the creator god and the sea monster. Much later, the Wisdom of Solomon will develop ideas about her role in creation, moving towards seeing Wisdom as divine and setting the stage for transformation into the 'Word' of our Gospel reading. This movement is by way of the 'dwelling' (tenting) of wisdom in Israel – just as the Word becomes flesh and dwells/ tents among 'his own' by whom he is rejected.

The glory of creation is again picked up in the Psalm – which preserves colour from ancient nature-mythology to serve the idea that God has created the world to do his will and reveal his glory: a thought which gives meaning to all our exploration, scientific and creative endeavour. It was the extraordinary strength of belief in the goodness of God's creation that transformed the old chaos-monster into a pliant creature, frolicking in the delight both of itself and its maker.

The Colossian hymn draws a parallel between the work of creation and the work of reconciliation. Jesus Christ is the one who creates order out of the disorder that has crept into the universe. He is seen as the source of all created things. It may well be that the fashion was for syncretistic religion, and propaganda in Colossae was undermining Jesus's uniqueness. He alone is presented as the place of encounter with God and the focus of Christian identity.

★   ★   ★

The Sunday Next before Lent

2 Kings 2:1–12
Psalm 50:1–6
2 Corinthians 4:3–6
Mark 9:2–9

JUST as the disciples *en route* for Jerusalem were granted a vision of Jesus as the place of meeting with God, so we are offered this story of the Transfiguration. Moses and Elijah pale into insignificance beside his transfigured presence. Much of Mark's Gospel concerns Jesus as the new Elisha/Elijah and as the new Moses. This narrative presents a vision of Jesus in heavenly glory as the Messiah and in continuity with the faith of Israel. It is sometimes suggested that this is a 'resurrection narrative' transposed by Mark to enhance the drama of the passion story. The starkness of Mark's resurrection account contrasts with those of the other Evangelists. Resurrection is experienced within the community only in its appropriation of the gospel. On this Sunday before Lent begins, here is a reminder of the glory to which Jesus is called, a vision to sustain the church through persecution and the dereliction of the cross.

The story of the ascension of Elijah and of the commissioning of Elisha provides the Old Testament parallel. For the editors of Kings the commissioning of Elisha is the main point of the story. By it he is authenticated as the true successor of Elijah upon whom both the work and the authority of the master have descended. Moses, under God, founded the covenant people. Both Elijah and Elisha were his successors in that their work was to ensure the continuance of that people in their own time.

The ascension of Elijah gained prominence later: Elijah was so close to God in spirit that he was taken to heaven without passing through the experience of death. In this he was linked with the patriarch Enoch, and both stories were seen by New Testament writers as foreshadowing the ascension of Jesus.

★

37

Perhaps Paul has been accused by the Corinthians of 'veiling' the gospel in some way. Clearly he is being undermined by others in Corinth and is responding to a challenge to his authority. In our passage he seems to be setting his ministry out on the grand scale, maintaining its superiority on account of the Spirit. The veil (which Moses put over his face) is now taken away because the Lord who spoke to Moses is present in the Spirit. Paul's gospel power, he claims, is from God – and is not veiled except to those whose minds are already blinded. Psalm 50, set for the Canticle, describes God 'shining forth' out of Zion to summon the earth to judgment at the end of time. First to be judged are his own people. They have brought sacrifices in abundance, but God's demand is for thanksgiving and prayer.

★ ★ ★

Ash Wednesday

Joel 2:1–2, 12–17 *or* Isaiah 58:1–12
Psalm 51:1–18
2 Corinthians 5:20b–6:10
Matthew 6:1–6, 16–21 *or* John 8:1–11

ALL too often Lent is far too dreary. Jesus's instruction to his disciples not to look dismal reminds us that Lent is a preparation for Easter. We are preparing to baptize new Christians; in former times we might have been expecting also to welcome back into fellowship those who had been separated from us by 'grievous sin'. Most importantly, we are looking forward to being raised from the dead, to the central feast of the Christian year. How then do we justify wearing long faces and refusing to enjoy parties, or flowers, or weddings?

The question is to identify where our treasure is, for there will also be our heart. The context of this saying is of Jesus's teaching about giving to charity, about praying and about fasting. It suggests that 'treasure upon earth, where moth and rust consume, and where thieves break in and steal', is the superficial glitter of public acclaim for correct religious observance. It is no more than the ephemeral reward of outward show, and it leads easily to hypocrisy, for it is not difficult to put on a show when the heart is elsewhere.

So the observation, 'where your treasure is, there your heart will be also', is no more than common sense. What you consider to be of most value will be the thing that occupies your thinking, and that will determine your motivation, and that will govern your behaviour. Jesus wants not an occasional show of piety, but a constant, year-on-year, dependable thirst for righteousness.

We might begin to identify our treasure by asking, 'What would a good Easter look like?' There is no more virtue in gaining a reputation for abstinence during Lent than there is in being known as able to hold our drink on Easter Day. But what is it that we really hope for? Having identified that, we might set our sight on making it real.

Such reflections will make for differences after Easter, too. If we are determined to 'know Christ and the power of his resurrection', it is possible that we shall not avoid 'sharing in his sufferings by becoming like him in his death'. We might fail, we might 'sin', we might have to ask forgiveness for not accomplishing what we set out to do; but we shall be on the way to discovering where our treasure is.

The passage from John – to be found in different places in the New Testament, according to some manuscripts – tells the powerful story of a woman presented to Jesus as deserving death for her adultery. It represents a tradition (a) of Jesus's consistent compassion, (b) of his intolerance of hypocrisy and (c) of his rather cavalier attitude to the Law. The woman can only 'go and sin no more' if she truly knows that she is forgiven. Our quest for holiness this Lent is also based upon the innocence which God has already declared on our behalf in the cross and resurrection of Jesus. To know that more deeply is now our aim.

★   ★   ★

The First Sunday of Lent

Genesis 9:8–17
Psalm 25:1–10
1 Peter 3:18–22
Mark 1:9–15

THE story of Noah features in the Hebrew scriptures as a means of establishing the relationship between God and all people. Unlike what happens later with Moses and Abraham, this covenant does not depend upon any action on the part of the human partner. God's promise is to all people on the earth, and the rainbow is the sign of his undertaking to guarantee the natural order, so that men and women may live on the earth and expect the seasons to come and go, the crops to grow and the food cycle to be maintained. The whole story is dependent upon that of the Flood; but the new relationship with humanity marks a new beginning for God and humankind, for God perceives that there is something endemic in the human race, the corollary of its being created in his image, which implies the necessity of rebellion alongside that of compliance in its relationship with God.

The Psalmist sings of God's faithfulness, but his understanding of this arises from his conscious awareness of a relationship within a covenant. On that basis he is able to recall God's dependability in rescue, forgiveness and sound instruction. Remembering the constant compassion of God enables him to look to the future with the assurance that God's goodness does not change. Doubtless Noah, for all his sense of blessing and thanksgiving, would have found it difficult to forget what had happened to all his friends and neighbours.

The First Letter of Peter uses the story of Noah as a prefiguring of baptism. Just as Noah and his family were saved through water, so those who are baptized are rescued from the power of sin and death. The Letter rejects the view that baptism is an image of washing, even though the suggestion is made in the very denial. What is more important is what the water of baptism signifies.

There is some debate about this: it means either (a) 'an appeal for a good conscience', or (b) 'a pledge on the basis of a good conscience'. If baptism is the former, it constitutes a request that God will grant a good conscience in spite of the sins which are endemic to the human condition. (It is likely that 'the spirits in prison' here are not the souls of the departed, but the spirits of all human beings which in this world are imprisoned by sin and death.) In this case, baptism is something done within the Christian community which calls upon God to maintain the faithfulness that he has displayed in the past. If baptism is a 'pledge', then the onus is subsequently on the person baptized and on the community which does the baptizing to hold fast to the pledge which they make.

Either is possible. It might be tempting for us to assert the primacy of the grace of God and therefore the necessity of maintaining that it is God's faithfulness which is the issue here; but, on the other hand, the commitment to holy living has to be undertaken in good faith by all who would follow Christ. Our promises to God are as important as God's promises to us; it is as we make them and seek to keep them that we discover, both the presence of his grace in enabling us to keep them, and the realization that it was grace which made it possible for us to make them at all.

This paradox is continued in the Gospel. For St Mark, Jesus, as the Son of God, is a paradoxical figure. On the one hand he is the one who is patient, or passive; that is in the strict grammatical sense of one who undergoes the actions of others. On the other hand he is active in bringing about what comes to be and in instigating what happens. The story of his baptism is his arrival on the dramatic scene both of his engagement with God in the world, and of his engagement with the world for God.

We are told very starkly where he comes from, 'from Nazareth of Galilee', and why he comes, 'to be baptized by John'. What happens there indicates that, from the start, he is marked out by God as God's own; but the implications of this, just as was the case with the nation of Israel, God's chosen and beloved (cf. Isaiah 42:1), is that the relationship is to start in the wilderness, as in Exodus 19. The Marcan narrative is nothing if not stark – some would even say, bleak. This is how the earliest of the Evangelists told the story of Jesus; and it represents an important antidote to many of our assumptions about 'gentle Jesus' and the 'sabbath rest by Galilee'. When God engages with humanity, there is struggle and hardship involved. The Son of God is called and commissioned by the Father to do the Father's will; only in the doing of it will he know himself to be the Son. It is the same for us who, this Lent, follow in his steps.

★　★　★

The Second Sunday of Lent

Genesis 17:1–7,15–16
Psalm 22:23–31
Romans 4:13–25
Mark 8:31–38

T HE call of Abraham was not a once-for-all affair. After he had been urged to leave his country and his kindred, to go to a land which God would show him, he remained at the call of God, who spoke to him in order to give him further directions for the conduct of his life. Here he receives the promise from God that he will have an heir, and that from his descendants will spring even kings. These stories of Abraham serve to remind us that our faith is rooted in the initiative which God takes to establish a relationship with the human race. It is for us to respond to him.

The Psalm, one of prayer and faith in the face of opposition, focuses upon God's faithfulness. It is the continuation of that Psalm which begins, 'My God! My God! Why have you forsaken me?', which, according to Mark 15:34, were the last words of Jesus from the cross. In this section the Psalmist records a determination to continue to sound God's praises even in the context of death and destruction; vindication is assumed.

The Letter to the Romans is not one of the easiest of texts with which to come to terms, but it repays serious and applied study. Paul's argument here focuses on the fact that Abraham was

42

promised an heir before he obeyed God's command to be circumcised. Paul deduces from this that promise comes before Law, and therefore the true children of Abraham are not so much those who keep the Law, but rather those who believe God's promise. For Paul, the primary promise is that those who believe in God are reckoned by him to be righteous – whatever they may have done.

The Gospel passage tells of Jesus foretelling his own death. His sharp words to Peter are consonant with his, perhaps curious, desire that the disciples should not tell anyone of his identity – which Peter had just confessed. Verses 34–38 are addressed not only to the disciples but also to the readers. The way of discipleship – the only way to life – is the way of the cross. As then, so now.

★   ★   ★

The Third Sunday of Lent

Exodus 20:1–17
Psalm 19
1 Corinthians 1:18–25
John 2:13–22

THE trouble with reading the Ten Commandments without any preface is that it isolates them from their context, both in the pages of scripture and in the life of the people of Israel. This dislocation – typified in some Christian traditions in having them inscribed on the walls of churches – has led to the belief in some circles that we need to 'preach the Law' before we can 'preach the gospel'. This approach runs the danger of implying that people must be made to feel as guilty as possible before they are offered the chance of forgiveness.

Such an attitude is far from valid. The Ten Commandments are part of a covenant, and they function as the sign of a relationship with God in which God takes the initiative, in which God guarantees the future and in which God sets out the possibilities by which the relationship may be maintained. These commands were not given either to make people feel how wretched they were at their inability to keep them, nor to indicate that keeping them will ensure God's begrudging favour. They were given as a sign that God delighted in the company of men and women, and that a certain way of life was required if they were to keep their part of this relationship with a God who acted morally in saving them from slavery. So it is that the people of Israel are obliged to regard all their relationships with God and with one another as rooted in this faith. God's choice of them has implications, both for their relationships with him and for their relationships with each other.

It is because the Law (of which the Ten Commandments are a part) symbolized the nation's relationship with a gracious yet demanding God that the Psalmist is able to speak – or sing – of it in the context of praise. The beauty of the skies, the passing of time and the radiant light of the sun bear silent yet clear testimony to the glory of God. The Law he has given to his people is every bit as eloquent, as enlightening, as searching and as delightful as they. What better way to please him than to keep its demands? And what could be worse than straying from its requirements?

In 1 Corinthians Paul is asserting the centrality of the cross in Christian preaching, in order to defend before the Christians at Corinth, not only his credentials, but also his behaviour and attitude. He says that the message of the cross is superior, not only to the unceasing search for meaning which the scribes pursued in their endless exegesis of the text of scripture, but also to the 'love of wisdom' (the Greek word for which is *philosophy*) for which the Greeks were renowned.

Clearly there is an element of exaggeration in this rhetoric, for Paul himself justified his preaching on the basis of scripture; he also had a hand in extending it. Christian faith since his time has developed as a faith grounded in texts. Nor are Christian life and behaviour set against thinking and the pursuit of what is wise. The important thing for Paul is that all these things are to be found in Christ, who sums them up and enables both scribe and thinker to see Christ in and through all things – and as sharing human pain with and, in some sense, on behalf of, humankind. The point is the universality of the good news of Jesus Christ, which is based upon his having died 'for all', whether Jews or Greeks. To this good news Paul is committed, and he has no objection whatever to being thought foolish for devoting his life to proclaiming it.

It is striking that John's Gospel has the story of the 'cleansing of the Temple' towards the beginning of the public life of Jesus. In the Synoptic Gospels (Matthew, Mark and Luke) it is placed at the end, and it provides the beginning of the major conflict that issues in Jesus's arrest, trial and crucifixion. However, John sets out the whole of the story of Jesus as a dramatic conflict between Jesus, the Logos, who is also the Light that has come into the world, and the 'powers of darkness', symbolized by 'the Jews'. For John this antagonism has its origin before the creation of the world.

The significant features of the story in John are (a) the way in which the Temple becomes a metaphor for Christ's body and (b) that it is the resurrection that gives force to this retelling of the story, with all its nuances and allusions. The conflict between light and darkness is joined, but the readers of this Gospel know that the outcome is already decided: the darkness will not master the light.

★   ★   ★

The Fourth Sunday of Lent

Numbers 21:4–9
Psalm 107:1–3, 17–22
Ephesians 2:1–10
John 3:14–21

THE rather curious story from the Book of Numbers tells of the reversal of the attitude of the Israelites which is recorded in Exodus 14.31, 'So the people feared the Lord, and they believed in the Lord and in his servant, Moses.' Here (v. 5) 'the people spoke against God and against Moses'. Their complaint was self-contradictory: the food is both 'no food' and 'miserable food'. The word *seraphim*, the plural of *seraph*, which may be translated 'poisonous' or 'fiery', can also be a synonym of the word *nachash*, which means 'serpent'. The adjective presumably refers to the effect of the serpent's bite. The cure for this wound is an example of mimetic magic, and it is repeated in the words of the text, for the word 'bronze' is *nechosheth*, a play on the word for serpent. It was the serpent in Genesis 3 who was the agent of human rebellion. Now serpents are used as punishment for Israel's rebellion.

Appropriately, Psalm 107 is a repetition of the theme of God's gracious acts in forgiveness. It recalls those events in Israel's history, such as the one we have just read, when the people complained and rebelled against God, and he was gracious to them and forgave them for their sins.

Ephesians is a restatement of forgiveness. This passage is part of a long 'Thanksgiving', in which the writer, probably not Paul himself, gives thanks for the reconciliation achieved both between heaven and earth and between God and humanity. The important feature seems to be that the believers have been given life again. They were dead in 'trespasses and sins', but 'together with Christ' they have been made alive, raised and seated – and the verbs all emphasize togetherness with God. Their status is now that of God's 'creation' – the word used is the origin of our word 'poem' – and the purpose of this creation is that they may perform the 'good works' which have been prepared for them.

The Gospel picks up the serpent theme. Here is a Pharisee who is not 'a Jew', in the Johannine sense of an opponent of the light. After the conflict in John 2 concerning the Temple, Nicodemus comes to Jesus and becomes the first in a line of individual Jews in Christian writing who are not part of the corporate race first demonized by John. Here Jesus refers to the serpent story to make a general point about the gospel. He himself will be 'lifted up', and those who look in faith to him will be cured of the wounds effected by the serpent of darkness and evil.

Is it Jesus or the narrator speaking at the end of the chapter? There is little difference, for – and John is not alone in this – Jesus is the mouthpiece of the Evangelist's theology. Death is represented as hatred of the light, and everlasting life is obtainable through faith in the Son.

★   ★   ★

Mothering Sunday

Exodus 2:1–10 *or* 1 Samuel 1:20–28
Psalm 34:11–20 *or* Psalm 127:1–4
2 Corinthians 1:3–7 *or* Colossians 3:12–17
Luke 2:33–35 *or* John 19:25b-27

MOTHERING Sunday is about returning to the 'mother church', that is, the church where we were baptized, in order to give thanks for our baptism. It is therefore a recollection of the beginning. This has become associated with visiting our mothers (and bringing simnel cake!) and expressing affection and thanks for what they have done in providing life, sustenance and support throughout life.

The Old Testament lessons speak of mothers: the mother of Moses, who is unnamed, and Hannah, the mother of Samuel. It was Moses who brought about deliverance of Israel from Egypt, and Samuel brought order out of the chaos of the time of the Judges by anointing the kings of the undivided kingdom, Saul and David. The implication of this choice of readings is that Judeo-Christian tradition owes much to these two mothers.

The story in Exodus 2 is of a canny mother and sister, who so arrange the nursing of Moses when he is found by Pharaoh's daughter that he is brought up by his own mother before being adopted as the son of Pharaoh's daughter. (All male children were to be killed, on the orders of Pharaoh.) The name given to Moses is a play on words. 'Moses' (the name may be of Egyptian origin) comes from a root, M-S-Y, meaning 'to be born'. The Hebrew root M-SH-H means 'to draw out (of water)'. Moses is found in

47

the river and 'drawn out' of it; but this pun also prefigures the 'drawing out' of water which will take place for all the Israelites at the Red Sea.

Another mother/son story is told in 1 Samuel 1. Elkanah had two wives, of whom Hannah was his favourite; but she was barren. She prayed for a child, and the priest who saw and heard her praying thought that she was either mad or drunk. Now she goes back, with the child, to the house of the Lord at Shiloh and pays her vow and hands Samuel over to Eli. The text also implies that it was Elkanah who went back with Samuel, having presumably taken full responsibility for his wife's vow.

Psalm 34 is a Wisdom Psalm, in which Wisdom is depicted as a wise mother instructing her son, giving him advice to ensure that he lives a long and prosperous life. It speaks of the virtue of reflection on life and on how it should be lived. Psalm 127 speaks of the joy of having children and the asset they are to the household. It is almost sensual in its talk of bed and sleep; maybe the point is that what goes on before the beloved is given sleep is what produces the children who are 'a heritage from the Lord' and the 'gift' from the fruit of the womb.

All this is grist to the 'family' mill. 2 Corinthians, however, in raising the notion of the 'consolation' which God provides, and Colossians in talking of the need to adopt loving attitudes towards our neighbour, move us towards the more negative aspects of family experience: death, separation, division and the re-ordering of domestic relationships and priorities which are consequent upon and focused in the presence of Jesus in the world, within a family and among humankind.

Colossians 3 (possibly by Paul, possibly not) speaks of the image of clothing, probably from a baptismal context, and lists the virtues to be expected of Christians. Nevertheless the nature of the advice remains firmly centred on Christ.

As with the Psalms, there is something not entirely satisfactory about the abbreviated portions chosen for the Gospel passages. That from Luke is the end of the Presentation narrative, when

48

Simeon has spoken the Nunc Dimittis and goes on to warn of the future and the pain that his prophecy inevitably entails. He notes that this will bring pain to Jesus's parents, too.

In John 19 the scene is at the cross. This is the story of how Mary came to be revered in the church as the adoptive parent of the Beloved Disciple; certainly it is probably more than the Lord's compassion for his mother at the end of his life; early respect for the memory of Mary may be reflected here.

★   ★   ★

The Fifth Sunday of Lent

Jeremiah 31:31–34
Psalm 51:1–12 *or* Psalm 119:9–16
Hebrews 5:5–10
John 12:20–33

THE covenant established in the time of Moses between God and the people of Israel was characterized ostensibly by the fact that the people willingly responded to God's initiative in entering into covenant relationship with them. They were to keep their part of the covenant by obeying the Law which was part of it. Over the years their disobedience, which resulted in their punishment and exile, became so offensive to God that he now offers a new kind of covenant, in which their response will be automatic. The Law of God will be written in their hearts, so that they will need neither reminders of it, nor threats nor encouragement to keep it.

In Psalm 51 the Psalmist prays for forgiveness and sees all his wrongdoing in the light of his relationship to God. This is traditionally associated with David's adultery with Bathsheba (2 Samuel 11–12)

Psalm 119 continues the Psalmist's praise of the Law. By delighting in what God commands the writer retains his standing before God.

Included here are the affective responses to that which symbolizes the relationship; the mental attitude which decides how to behave; and the will to do what is right.

The passage from Hebrews 5 continues the Epistle's exploration of the theme of Christ's superiority over what preceded him in Jewish tradition. Here the contrast is with the office of High Priest. Verse 5 says that he did not seek the office himself, with all its glory, but was appointed to it by God; his calling to be God's Son made him *de facto* God's High Priest – by placing the texts together Christ's superiority to the Levitical High Priesthood is founded, for Hebrews, in the story of the High Priest of Salem, in Genesis 14, who came out to meet and honour Abraham after his victory over the kings in the Valley of Siddim.

The Epistle to the Hebrews makes firmer the link between sonship and priesthood by associating obedience with suffering. The sacrificial offering which Christ made was his own flesh (Hebrews 7:27, 9:14), and that offering was the means of his own sanctification. As the greatest of priests he is now able to offer salvation for all who are obedient to him.

For the author of the Fourth Gospel the moment at which Greeks come to seek out Jesus with the desire to meet him is the sign for him that his time has come. Jesus has come into the world for all peoples, Greeks (i.e. Gentiles) as well as Jews. John's drama of light and darkness is conceived on a cosmic scale; and the new life which Jesus offers is for all people. The background of thought in John's Gospel is as universal as is the message the Gospel promotes.

But it is only by the sacrifice of himself that Jesus will obtain eternal life for all who follow him, so he must prepare to give his life in death; this is to be his moment of glory. This is one of the many moments in John's Gospel which seem to pick up the theme of the Transfiguration in the Synoptic tradition. The name of God is glorified again and again; in this Gospel, in the life of Jesus and in the continuing life of the human community.

The death is to be by means of his being 'lifted up' (an echo of last Sunday's 'lifting up' of the serpent). Crucifixion is the means by which this will happen.

★ ★ ★

Palm Sunday
Liturgy of the Palms

Mark 11:1–11 *or* John 12:12–16
Psalm 118:1–2, 19–24

CHARACTERISTICALLY Mark's story of Jesus's approach to Jerusalem leaves open the question as to whether the finding of the colt was a miracle of intelligence or some pre-arranged deal and signal. The names of the villages, Bethphage and Bethany, give local precision to the story; they may also reflect an element of symbolism; they mean, respectively, 'house of figs' and 'house of dates'; both are a Hebrew image of plenty and prosperity, yet Jesus had used the image of a fig tree as a prophetic sign of judgment.

His 'looking around at everything' implies his ownership of it. Mark has quoted Malachi 3:1 at the beginning of the Gospel: 'See, I am sending my messenger to prepare the way before me . . .' Here the quotation may be said to continue: '. . . and the Lord whom you seek will suddenly come to his temple. The messenger of the covenant in whom you delight – indeed, he is coming, says the Lord of hosts. But who can endure the day of his coming, and who can stand when he appears?' The coming of Jesus to Jerusalem, according to Mark, signifies the coming of God to judgment.

In John it is the crowd, not the disciples, who take the initiative in holding palm branches and singing 'Hosannah'; and Jesus himself finds the young donkey, in fulfilment of the prophecy from Zechariah 9:9. There is no indication at all of how it is found.

The disciples here are only remarkable for their lack of understanding; the Gospel nevertheless puts the whole incident in the context

51

of resurrection faith by stating, 'when Jesus was glorified, then they remembered that these things had been written of him and had been done to him'. Again we recall that the whole story of Jesus makes sense only in the light of his resurrection.

Psalm 118 is a Psalm of thanksgiving for an annual pilgrimage to Jerusalem. It carries a number of themes which are appropriate to this day: opening the gates; stones and cornerstones; approaching the altar; and thanksgiving. Read in the light of the intentions of Jesus, we may say that thanksgiving is due from the people of God who depend upon the readiness of Jesus to enter the holy city in order to offer himself in sacrifice, but a grim sense of foreboding must colour our reading of it as we consider how Jesus might have understood his approach to the city.

★　　★　　★

Palm Sunday
Liturgy of the Passion

Isaiah 50:4–9a
Psalm 31:9–16
Philippians 2:5–11
Mark 14:1–15:47 *or* Mark 15:1–39 *or* Mark 15:1–47

THE passage from Isaiah 50 echoes a theme to be found in Isaiah 53, of suffering willingly accepted and offered. Faith is not about a morbid masochism, however, nor about seeking out suffering for its own sake. Rather, it has to do with the realism that suffering is unavoidable, and that it may become redemptive, when it is offered to God in hopeful anticipation of the eventual creation of compassion.

The Psalmist prays for mercy because of the trouble in which he finds himself. Grief, sighing and affliction are his present lot, but his trust remains firm: 'My times are in your hand' is the prayer of all who have sought solace in the divine pity for all that they have had to endure.

Philippians 2 speaks – or rather, sings, for this is an early Christian hymn – of the glory of Christ in humbling himself as a slave, assuming human flesh and giving his life to the point of death. His exaltation by resurrection was the vindication of a whole life poured out in obedience to God, in order to show that this is how God himself is with his people.

Mark's Passion narrative continues this theme. The reader should note the identification of the two feasts of Passover and Unleavened Bread; in fact they were different, even though the former followed immediately upon the latter. Nevertheless the identification underlines the incongruity of the obsession of 'the chief priests and the scribes' with finding a way to do away with Jesus.

The anointing at Bethany foreshadows Jesus's burial; note that the name is not given of the person who complained at the waste of money. It is this that inspires Judas Iscariot to betray Jesus to the authorities.

The preparations for the Passover recall the preparations for the entry to Jerusalem; is this a miracle of provision, or is it part of a pre-arranged plan? We are not told. The meal itself is dominated by two things: first, Jesus's assertion that one of his disciples will betray him; second, by his taking of the bread and the cup, blessing them and distributing them, after placing his own interpretation upon them, and then taking a vow of abstinence until the kingdom of God should come.

Again, Jesus makes a stark prediction of what is about to happen – albeit in coded form – and foretells his resurrection. Peter's denial is indicated, along with his protestations, in which all the disciples join. The reader knows better than they.

Gethsemane sees Jesus take with him the intimate three (Peter, James and John), and pray that 'this cup' (of what he is about to go through) might be removed from him. After praying thus he finds his companions asleep; the fact that this happens three times suggests that their failure to 'be there for him' (as the modern jargon has it) is total. After the third occasion the betrayer and the crowd from the Jewish authorities are there to arrest him. His identity is sealed with a kiss from Judas; one member of the crowd has his ear cut off by an enthusiastic disciple, and then all the disciples flee.

Who is the 'young man' in a linen cloth? We are not told; the only other mention of a linen cloth in Mark is of that which Joseph of Arimathea bought in which to wrap Jesus's body. Is this a hint of a kind of resurrection for others at the point at which the Son of God is to be condemned to death?

The trial, such as it is, proceeds – though it would not have been legal at night – but Jesus refuses to answer any question put to him, until he admits that he is 'the Messiah, the Son of the Blessed One'. The Jews condemn him to death, and now have to persuade Pilate to concur. Meanwhile, Peter is occupied in fulfilling his Master's prophecy, falling headlong into whose trap, that of the serving maid or of Jesus? His bitter regret will be met at the resurrection by his specific inclusion among the disciples who are to return to Galilee (Mark 16:7).

Pilate, the governor, tries to prevaricate and have Jesus released by means of the observance of a popular custom. This attempt fails, and he simply goads the crowds and insults them; they, in turn, refuse to answer his questions. But he gives in.

The soldiers mock Jesus – and, by implication, the Jews, since the soldiers regard him as the Jews' king. A passer-by, identified as a relation of someone known to the earliest readers of the Gospel, is forced to carry the cross to the place of crucifixion, where the ghastly sentence is carried out.

The process lasts for three hours, which Pilate later reckons to be rather quick. There are those who pity him, there are those who mock him, there are those who simply watch, and there are those who are moved by the event. Among those who care for him are the women who, with the help of Joseph of Arimathea, will bury him – and who will later find his tomb empty. They are to discover, like the reader, that this is not the end of the story.

★   ★   ★

The Monday of Holy Week

Isaiah 42:1–9
Psalm 36:5–11
Hebrews 9:11–15
John 12:1–11

THE readings in Holy Week intertwine the Servant Songs from Second Isaiah with passages from the Epistles. Alongside these are placed readings from John 12, 13 and 18, the last hours of Jesus's life as John's drama presents it.

The Servant of Isaiah 42 is one who enjoys God's special favour. He bears God's spirit and acts on God's behalf. His godly actions, however, are gentle, and his purpose is to establish justice. In addressing him, God speaks of his own creative power. The implication is that this creativity is the very same that is at work in the call of the Servant and that, consequently, the work which the Servant assumes on God's behalf will be similarly creative.

In the context established by this eulogy the Psalmist speaks of God's love and faithfulness. Those who are his people may expect to enjoy the abundance of his provision.

In the Epistle to the Hebrews we are treading on very different ground. Here the imagery is not of the gentleness, grace and dependency of God's purposes, but of priesthood, bloody sacrifices and an understanding of Christ within the sacrificial system of the Jerusalem Temple. The particular point is that those ancient practices – no longer offered once the Temple was destroyed forty years after the crucifixion of Jesus – were, in a spiritual sense, superseded by the death of Jesus on the cross. The argument runs thus: Jesus Christ is God's Son as well as his High Priest. The offering he makes is therefore infinitely superior to the temporal system bound to the Jewish Temple. The covenant ratified by the shedding of his blood fulfils all the requirements of the first covenant and brings 'the promised eternal inheritance' of complete forgiveness of everybody for all sins they have committed.

It is almost as though the story in John 12 presupposes an understanding, both of the grace and faithfulness of the God who appoints the Servant to do his will and of the Christ who sacrificed himself for the forgiveness of the whole world. Unwittingly, Mary's love, expressed in very blatant and sensual terms, takes on a profound spiritual meaning; her love for him expresses what might be all human response to his love for the world. There always will be those, like Judas, who whinge at every expense of loving. Is not this, too, a kind of betrayal? However, such meanness is put into context both by the estimate of the one loved and by the depth of the love expressed. Doesn't any lover wish to expend a bank vault on the loved one – and regret only that it might be too paltry a gift?

★　　★　　★

The Tuesday of Holy Week

Isaiah 49:1–7
Psalm 71:1–14
1 Corinthians 1:18–31
John 12:20–36

TODAY's Servant speaks as though he were a prophet called like Isaiah (cf. Isaiah 6) or Jeremiah (cf. Jeremiah 1), with no option but to respond to the imperious command of God who knows him from the moment of conception and decrees what his vocation is to be. This Servant is to have the capacity for incisive speech and accurate address, even though there is a hint that his message will go unheeded: 'I have spent my strength for nothing and vanity.'

But there is more. The Servant is not to have a task restricted simply to the interests of Israel; he is to be a light for all the nations.

Rulers across the world are to regard him as the agent of rescue and well-being for all people.

Psalm 71 is a prayer for protection and vindication. There is an atmosphere of anxiety here, as though the Psalmist were under attack from some enemy. It is not given to us to know whether these foes are imaginary or physical – and that does not appear to be the point. Trust in God is the Psalmist's only resource; in God he fully expects support, and, eventually, vindication.

In 1 Corinthians Paul asserts the subversive simplicity of the cross. Its apparent folly contrasts with the Greek pursuit of wisdom. 'Philosophy' means 'love of wisdom', and the Greeks were renowned for that. The cross also contrasts with the need for 'signs'. Paul had been asked to demonstrate the signs which would authenticate his apostleship, just as Jesus had been asked for a sign of his authority. In their context here, both of these attitudes demonstrate an unwillingness to have faith without guarantees of certainty (which would mean absence of faith). Not that there is anything wrong with the pursuit of wisdom or an interest in signs! The point is that these evasions of faith also avoid confrontation with suffering and the possibility that it might be redemptive, that God's purposes might be disclosed within it, as the resurrection of Jesus demonstrates.

Clearly these first believers in Corinth were not renowned for their high birth or their sophistication, and for Paul this was a further mark of God's preference for the matter-of-fact and the physical, rather than for abstractions and evasions. This is sufficient guarantee for him that the appeal of the cross is universal; pain and suffering are universal, and those whose lives are transfigured by faith in Christ know no boundaries of wealth or birth, neither are they restrained by restrictive traditions.

John's Gospel, after the anointing at Bethany and the entry into Jerusalem, notes that there were Greeks in Jerusalem for the festival of the Passover. It is when some of these begin to enquire after Jesus that he decides that 'his hour' has come. There are a number of occasions in the Fourth Gospel when events take place which echo the Transfiguration traditions in the Synoptic Gospels, and this is one such.

Jesus's decision that his hour has come causes him to realize that this 'hour' will be one of pain. He prays, almost not knowing what to pray, and wonders whether he should ask to be delivered from the very 'hour' to which his whole life has tended. But no; he will ask the Father to 'glorify his name', and a voice from heaven assures him that this is the divine purpose. God's name will be glorified; that is, his character will be vindicated, when the conflict is joined in which evil will be defeated, and the idea of being 'lifted up' indicates the nature of this struggle for victory. Once this victory is secure, there will be no opportunity for those who sided with evil to change sides. The judgment (for that is what 'crisis' means) will sort out those who belong to the light from those who belong to darkness.

★　　★　　★

The Wednesday of Holy Week

Isaiah 50:4–9a
Psalm 70
Hebrews 12:1–3
John 13:21–32

THE Servant in Isaiah 50 speaks of his own experience. His skill and calling are to teach, which he further defines as 'sustaining the weary with a word'; content and relationship are held together. What follows suggests that what he says is not always acceptable to his hearers. But he lays claim to an integrity which does not rebel when opposition arises; he 'gives his back to those who strike him' and does not hide his face from insult and spitting. He may therefore expect vindication from the Lord who called him.

Psalm 70 may be read as the prayer of such a Servant. A belief in ultimate vindication does not remove the desire to pray for it;

rather, it intensifies the relationship between Lord and Servant, which is dependent now not upon the certain reward, but on the mutuality of trust and dependability.

A further angle on this relationship is perceived in the lesson from Hebrews 12. Here the 'witnesses' are all the heroes of Jewish faith who have proved their faithfulness, and their praise is sung in Hebrews 11. The Epistle urges its readers to note the presence of these while keeping the eyes focused on Jesus, who is the beginning and the end, the pioneer and perfecter of faith. He kept his eye on the goal and attained what was promised him, namely the glory which was his due as the obedient Son and High Priest of God.

The Gospel presents us with Jesus 'troubled in spirit'. For John the trouble has a specific focus in the fact of his imminent betrayal; and the presence of the betrayer at table with him and all the disciples may remind the reader of the Psalm – 'but it was my own familiar friend . . .'. The general point from the Synoptic tradition, 'one of the twelve that dips with me in the dish', becomes in John the specific means by which the betrayer is identified. There is a striking quasi-sacramentalism in 'after Judas had received the bread, Satan entered into him' – but again, the disciples are prevented from seeing the true nature of what is happening among them. What Judas has to do is not give money to the poor – a custom at Passover – but receive money for the betrayal of the friend of the poor and become the Satanic agent of the resolution of the conflict which will bring about the world's salvation.

When we are told, 'And it was night . . .', we are being told more than the time; but, paradoxically, in the deepest darkness is sown the seed of glorious light.

★ ★ ★

Maundy Thursday

Exodus 12:1–4, 11–14 *or* Exodus 12:1–14
Psalm 116:1–2, 12–19
1 Corinthians 11:23–26
John 13:1–17, 31b–35

O N Maundy Thursday we take a break from the Servant Songs in favour of the Old Testament theme of the Passover, to which allusion is made in the Last Supper, and with the Eucharist. The story of the washing of the disciples' feet comprises a lesson which Jesus wants them to learn. It is one thing for him to be aware of what he is doing; quite another for them to have understood it too.

The passage from Exodus tells of the institution of the Passover; the lamb is to be eaten with reminders of the bitterness of slavery, and its blood is to be smeared on the lintels of the houses, to remind the Israelites that it was by the shedding of the blood of the firstborn of Egypt that their emancipation was achieved.

The choice of Psalm 116 for this day is not without its curiosity, but it has reference to the 'cup of salvation' and the observance of vows, which feature in the Synoptic accounts of the Last Supper.

Paul simply reminds his readers of the institution of the Lord's Supper, in order to urge them to maintain the unity of the Christian community; we might observe how this central rite has become the focus of so much division.

John, however, who does not regard the Last Supper as a Passover meal – for he has the crucifixion of Jesus taking place at the time of the slaughter of the Passover lambs – focuses upon a different aspect of that Supper.

Washing feet is a slave's job. What is significant here is that it is the host who performs it – and that in order to teach his disciples humility. For John, Jesus is the Logos – the Word – of God who has become flesh, and now walks the earth. He knows that the Father has given all things into his hands, and that he has come from God and is going to God. He knows also of the treachery of Judas and of the pain which the coming days will bring, so he 'gets up from the table, takes off his outer robe, ties a towel around himself, pours water into a basin and begins to wash the disciples' feet and to wipe them with the towel'.

This is the language of sacrifice, because it has to do with the act of sanctifying, of making holy what he has at his disposal – and that is the meaning of the Latin *sacrum ficere*, from which the word comes. The more we devote ourselves to God, the more precious to us will be the offerings which we make in sacrifice to him; and what is more precious to us than our pain? Is not this the last thing we are able to let go? In getting up from table to wash his disciples' feet, Jesus begins the sacrifice of what is to happen to him.

There is also the issue here of who Jesus is; and closely bound up with the identity of Jesus is always the question of the identity of his disciples. The washing which Jesus offers is not primarily about being clean; it is about being included. Hence Peter's problem. His refusal to have his feet washed can easily be explained, either as excessive humility, or as infuriating religiosity. However, we really do all belong together, for Jesus washes the whole human race, and the discovery of our identity lies in our acknowledgment of that truth.

★   ★   ★

Good Friday

Isaiah 52:13–53:12
Psalm 22
Hebrews 10:16–25 *or* Hebrews 4:14–16;5:7–9
John 18:1–19:42

THE Old Testament lesson comprises the final Servant Song, and we are left wondering who this Servant is. The song does seem, of course, to be particularly appropriate to the death of Jesus, and it is surprising that the New Testament does not make more use of it. However, if it is regarded as, in some sense, prophetic, we need to bear in mind that the concept of 'fulfilment' is a complex matter which requires theological imagination to make connections; not all the details of these songs are appropriate to Jesus, and we must be careful not to force the parallels. The question of the Servant's identity must first be asked within the context of Hebrew religion, for a hasty association of these passages with Jesus both fails to do them justice in their own right and risks missing important insights into how they are applied in later Christian tradition.

It appears that the Servant may be an individual; whether a prophet or a king – even a foreign one. He could also be the nation. Alternatively, the very variety and complexity may be deliberate, and draw attention, not so much to the identity of the Servant, but rather to the nature of God who is able to call all those characters to his service. The effect of this upon the interpretation of the final Servant Song is therefore most significant, for it indicates that there is close relationship between the Servant and God himself.

The theme of both lessons from the Epistle to the Hebrews embraces that of confidence; in chapters 4–5 is the encouragement to approach God in worship and prayer, especially in the context of human suffering, and in Hebrews 10 the implications of the sacrifice of Jesus are worked out; it is to produce good works in believers and, again, to encourage confidence before God.

John 18–19 presents a Passion narrative which is distinctive (as indeed, does Luke; Matthew follows Mark more closely), and these two chapters would repay careful study. We might note that there is no agony in the Garden, but we should recall John 12:27, when the Greeks come to see Jesus, and he refers to the universality of the cross as he is about to be rejected by the Jews. Jesus's question 'Who are you looking for?' is the same as that addressed to Mary Magdalene in the garden in John 20:15 – except that this instance is plural and that singular; the quest for Jesus both leads to his cross and to the discovery of him in his risen glory. The cross is to be the means, both of his glory, and of salvation for all people.

The quotation from the scriptures, 'I did not lose a single one of those whom you gave me', seems deliberately to contradict 'I will strike the shepherd, and the sheep will be scattered' in Mark 14:27. There are more details given about the cutting off of the ear of one of the soldiers: we are told his name, and we are told that it was Peter who did it. All these details heighten the drama. In Luke the disciples were told to take swords with them; here Jesus's response is a rebuke, as it is in Matthew.

We are told that Jesus was taken to Annas before Caiaphas, but not why, nor what happened there. Peter's denial takes place, with no further reference to it after the dramatic conclusion, 'And the cock crowed.' We should note that the issue of defilement is significant for John because unlike the timescale of the Synoptic Gospels, the Passover lambs have yet to be slaughtered.

Pilate attempts to have Jesus acquitted, but he fails. In presenting Jesus to them with the word, 'Here is your king', Pilate is taunting both Jesus and his accusers, and their conversation concerning 'truth' is full of irony, in that he does not know that Jesus has called himself 'the truth' in John 14:6. The crowd's claim, 'We have no king but Caesar!', is their final self-condemnation, and Pilate appears to have the last word in this battle of words with the inscription he has placed on the cross.

The name of the place, Golgotha, the place of the skull, is a macabre detail, and the casting lots for clothing echoes Psalm 22. The final reference to a 'garden' recalls both the beginning of chapter 18 and the gardener in John 20:15.

★   ★   ★

Easter Eve

Job 14.1–14 *or* Lamentations 3.1–9, 19–24
Psalm 31:1–4, 15–16
1 Peter 4:1–8
Matthew 27:57–66 *or* John 19:38–42

IN the light of all that Job has suffered – loss of land, of wealth, of prosperity, of health and of children – he reflects on the precariousness of life. This reflection is to be set alongside the hopeful assertions made elsewhere in scripture, and by people in happier circumstances. Here there is no glimmer of hope, and Job is the model of those who refuse to give in to sentimentalism. He is suffering unjustly, and will not compromise the truth of that fact. The Lamentations passage provides a contrast in that, though suffering is every bit as real, this text holds out the hope of some restoration, for the mercies of God are 'new every morning' (unless this is some form of bitter irony). The Psalmist prays for deliverance from all that has happened to him.

All these are appropriate expressions of a sense of desolation after Good Friday. It does no harm for the Christian community to stay with that sense of death – it is the experience of many.

1 Peter suggests that suffering, in the form of persecution, indicates a level of advancement in discipleship which shows that deliberate sinning is a thing of the past. The reference therefore is to what Christians used to do and to what 'Gentiles', i.e. non-believers, still continue to do. In any case, for this writer, suffering and death mean an end to sinning; this principle is extended to the view that Christ, in the realm of the dead, preached the gospel to the spirits of the dead, in order to bring them life in the spirit; it is assumed that the end of all things is near.

Matthew 27 has Joseph of Arimathea, now openly confessing his belief in Jesus, providing a tomb for his body. It is important that the burial take place before any ritual defilement is possible; Matthew wishes to remind his largely Jewish Christian community, though they have been expelled from the synagogue, that there is ritual impurity involved in the death of Jesus. We also have the first part of the story of the guard set over the tomb; this will provide an early example of polemic against Jewish claims that Jesus's disciples came and stole the body.

John 19 repeats the garden story; maybe because of its symbolic value for new life and resurrection. The word is used in the Septuagint for the garden of the Song of Songs, where bride and bridegroom meet. It also symbolizes in Third Isaiah the new relationship between God and Israel, for God both makes his people like a watered garden and places them in one. The Garden of Genesis 3 was the place from which humankind was excluded. After the resurrection the Garden becomes a place for restoration and inclusion.

★   ★   ★

Easter Vigil

A minimum of three Old Testament readings should be chosen. The reading from Exodus 14 should always be used.

Genesis 1:1–2.4a *with* Psalm 136:1–9, 23–26
Genesis 7:1–5, 11–18; 8:6–18; 9:8–13 *with* Psalm 46
Genesis 22:1–18 *with* Psalm 16
Exodus 14:10–31
Exodus 15:20–21 *with* Exodus 15:1b–13, 17–18
Isaiah 55:1–11 *with* Isaiah 12:2–6
Baruch 3:9–15, 32–4.4 *or* Proverbs 8:1–8, 19–21; 9:4b–6 *with* Psalm 19
Ezekiel 36:24–28 *with* Psalm 42 and 43
Ezekiel 37:1–14 *with* Psalm 143
Zephaniah 3:14–20 *with* Psalm 98
Romans 6:3–11
Psalm 114
Mark 16:1–8

I N the Easter vigil we watch with the grieving disciples, we walk with the women through the empty streets of Jerusalem in the hour before dawn, sharing their horror, loss, and confusion, and we bring to God a world which throbs with those feelings still. However, on behalf of that world – and for ourselves – we face those feelings with faith. The Lectionary provides a wonderful series of Old Testament passages which lead up to a powerful climax in the readings from Romans and Mark, proclaiming the resurrection of Christ. (Incidentally, provision is also made for these Old Testament passages to be read over the Sundays of Easter.)

How do we face horror, loss and confusion with faith? Reading Genesis 1, we remind ourselves that God has a good plan for his creation, that he intends order, not chaos; delight, not sorrow. (The Easter Vigil is the chief focus of thinking about creation in the Revised Common Lectionary, although the Anglican version of it has introduced a 'creation' day on the Second Sunday before Lent.)

To be created means to live with the tension between aspiration (to know the Creator on his paradise earth!) and actuality (that knowledge is denied daily by the barbarity and meanness to which we have sunk).

Reading the story of the Flood (Genesis 7–9), we remind ourselves that the Creator intervenes, that the world's hell-bent rush back to chaos will stop at his word, and that in the midst of disaster he is there to save the obedient.

Reading the story of the sacrifice of Isaac (Genesis 22), we reflect on God's hiddenness and presence. He shakes Abraham to the core by the command to sacrifice Isaac, tests his faith and love to the uttermost, then steps in with a last-minute deliverance. Similarly he was hidden from Christ on the cross, he is hidden behind the agonies of his world, and yet . . . there is grace at the last, secret, surprising, overwhelming.

Reading the story of the crossing of the Red Sea (Exodus 14), we reflect on the terror that a living faith sometimes involves. That nail-biting uncertainty over a diagnosis, that heart-stopping wait for exam results, that throat-drying public appearance, that humiliating apology – we've all been there, casting ourselves upon God for help like the Israelites with the Red Sea in front and the massed army of Egypt behind, and no escape . . . unless God steps in. And he does.

Reading the 'wisdom' passages (Proverbs 8 or Baruch 3–4), we think about God's secret presence in the world, in its order, its beauty, its complexity, its literature and art, in the scriptures, and supremely in Christ, who is the wisdom of God in Person.

Finally, reading the prophetic passages from Isaiah, Ezekiel and Zephaniah, we share their longing for deliverance from sin, for new life and a transformed heart – the longing that supremely paves the way for the coming of the Christ.

And so, as dawn breaks, we turn from all the sins, longings and imperfections of our world – from its horror, loss and confusion – to the new life won for us by Christ, and so wonderfully opened on Easter morning. Can we grasp it with something better than the incredulity which gripped the women (Mark 16:8)? Can we truly receive it, face the world and say 'But God . . .'?

★   ★   ★

Easter Day

Acts 10:34–43 *or* Isaiah 25:6–9
Psalm 118:1–2, 14–24
1 Corinthians 15:1–11 *or* Acts 10:34–43
John 20:1–18 *or* Mark 16:1–8

I N the New Testament passages set for this Day of Days (Acts 10, 1 Corinthians 15 and John 20), we are struck by the emphasis placed by all three on the fact of the resurrection. The Christian church has sometimes been tempted to think of the resurrection as a powerful symbolic story expressing the ultimate victory of good over evil, life over death, hope over despair – which can be called 'true' whether or not Jesus's body rose to life. There are many such symbolic stories in the Bible, usually called parables. But the resurrection is not presented as a story of that sort.

Peter calls himself a 'witness' of all the events surrounding Jesus, and lists the resurrection alongside everything else that happened to him. As an event, nothing distinguishes the resurrection from Jesus's preaching and healing ministry. It happened within history, and the disciples found themselves eating and drinking with Jesus just as they had done before he died (Acts 10:41).

Similarly Paul appeals to witnesses in his attempt to convince the Corinthian sceptics. Some Christians there were unhappy with the idea of bodily resurrection, preferring to 'spiritualize' it. But for Paul the bodily resurrection of Christ, as an event in space and time, is the vital heart of true Christian faith. So he asserts five things: (a) this is the historic faith he received (1 Corinthians 15:3–4), which (b) the Corinthians initially accepted (v. 11), and (c) the scriptures lead us to expect (v. 4); (d) the resurrection is a solid fact of history, attested by over 500 people (vv. 5–7), and (e) because of God's grace it has had an amazing impact on his own life, turning him into a passionate 'worker' for the Lord (vv. 8–10).

John's Gospel is sometimes called the 'spiritual' Gospel – a description that goes back to the late second-century writings of Clement of Alexandria. And John certainly gives us, overall, a more reflective presentation of Jesus. But he tells the story of the resurrection with such an eye for detail that he clearly wants us to believe that Jesus's body was miraculously raised to life and left the tomb.

Most intriguing is the significance which John attaches to the grave-wrappings. The Beloved Disciple (so-called) examines these carefully, providing a clear description of their condition and position (John 20:6–7), and as a result 'believes', even though he was not expecting a resurrection (vv. 8–9). Clearly John is prompting us to ask what it was that convinced this disciple.

We must remember that, if the tomb had been attacked by grave-robbers, they would have been interested in stealing the highly valuable spices and ointments, a hundred pounds of which had been given by Nicodemus and used in burying Jesus (John 19:39–40). Thus they would have stolen the wrappings, full of these ointments, and not left them behind. No grave-robbers would remove the wrappings and take the body. And in addition John describes their tidiness, particularly in the case of the cloth which had been tied around the head. It was still 'bound around itself' as it had been on Jesus's head – except that his head was no longer within it.

By emphasizing that both disciples saw this, John ensures their status as acceptable witnesses under Jewish law. The same is not true for Mary Magdalene, who now meets Jesus personally (vv. 11–18). But then that will always be the case: evidence can take us so far, but only a personal encounter with the risen Lord will end speculation and puzzlement. And Easter invites us into such an encounter!

★　★　★

The Second Sunday of Easter

Acts 4:32–35
Psalm 133
1 John 1:1–2:2
John 20:19–31

OUR Gospel from John 20, the second resurrection appearance in John, forms the centrepiece of today's readings. Just as Mary was commissioned, in the first appearance, to go and tell her fellow-disciples about the resurrection (John 20:17–18), so now all the disciples are commissioned to go and be witnesses. Jesus symbolically anoints them with the Holy Spirit, as he sends them into the world to continue his own mission from God (vv. 21–22).

And then the writer of this Gospel reveals that his own purpose in writing fits in with this commission (v. 31): though his readers cannot 'see' Jesus physically as Thomas did, dispelling all doubt, yet his plan is that they should 'believe' through reading the testimony he has summarized in the Gospel. He has focused on Jesus's 'signs', he tells us – perhaps with the resurrection as the last and greatest of these – because he thinks that they speak most clearly of Jesus's true identity as 'my Lord and my God!'

In the other readings we begin to see this commission being worked out. What does it mean, to bear testimony to our Lord Jesus Christ – to carry on his mission to the world? History soberly reminds us of many failures, of times when Christians have spoken a very different message from that of the Prince of Peace, the King of Love. But between them today's other readings point to the three essentials of true, consistent, Christian witness in the world:

(1) Lifestyle. The Psalm and the reading from Acts point together to the uniquely different lifestyle to which God's people are called. Psalm 133 celebrates that passionate unity of heart and mind which forgives all hurts, and goes on loving against the odds; such love, says the Psalmist, is the holiest thing of all, like the anointing oil which consecrated Aaron as High Priest. We see this mutual commitment in action in Acts 4:32–35 in a most practical way, challenging us today to set all our possessions at Christ's disposal, out of love for those in need around us. If a watching world sees this love between the disciples of Christ, it will speak volumes about our Master.

(2) Worship. The optional Old Testament reading (Exodus 14:10–31, 15:20–21) gives us the story of the deliverance of Israel at the Red Sea, finishing with Miriam leading the women in dance and praise (Exodus 15:20–21). The experience of God's rescue produces worship immediately. And the best worship is always like that; it arises straight from our own experience of the grace and presence of God, especially at times of trouble. If we worship like that, the world will notice.

(3) Witness. The lovely passage from 1 John – beginning a series of readings from this letter during the Easter season – gives us the other side of worship. If worship expresses back to God what he has done for us, then witness expresses it before others. The two go together, as the two halves of our response to grace. We cannot

70

keep quiet. And so John begins this letter with his testimony – 'what we have heard, what we have seen with our eyes . . .' (v. 1). And this quickly develops into a summary of the Christian message itself (vv. 5ff.), which we, too, must be ready to share with neighbours and friends, with simplicity and clarity, when opportunity arises.

★   ★   ★

The Third Sunday of Easter

Acts 3:12–19
Psalm 4
1 John 3:1–7
Luke 24:36b–48

Our Gospel reading follows on from the 'road to Emmaus' story, not just because of its position in Luke's Gospel but also in its basic message. Although the answer to the two friends' perplexity and sorrow was walking beside them on the road – the risen Jesus – they were not allowed to recognize him until he had 'interpreted to them the things about himself in all the scriptures' (Luke 24:27). Luke's message is clear: the church desperately needs the scriptures, if we are rightly to understand our experience of Christ. Better not to have the experience, than to have it and misinterpret it.

So now, at the end of that day, the risen Christ appears to all the disciples together, and rubs home the same message. In all that has happened to him, the scriptures have been fulfilled (v. 44). They must learn to reread the scriptures around him (v. 45), and this will enable them not only to understand what has happened to him (v. 46), but also to see what lies ahead for them (v. 47). They must play their part in the Grand Plan, announced by God in the scriptures, of bringing forgiveness and reconciliation to the whole world. Even the coming Holy Spirit has been promised in advance (v. 49), so they know what to wait for.

We meet this emphasis also in today's other reading from Luke's pen, Acts 3:12–19. Peter boldly tells his hearers that God even used the hostility of Jesus's enemies to fulfil his plan: 'In this way God fulfilled what he had foretold through all the prophets, that his Messiah would suffer' (v. 18). By calling Jesus God's 'servant' (v. 13), Peter recalls the prediction of the 'suffering servant of the Lord' in Isaiah 53, and this is probably one of the chief scriptures in mind.

What are we to make of this emphasis on the role of the scriptures in the church? We can think about it from two angles, addressing two equal and opposite pitfalls which have often trapped unwary Christians. On the one hand, church history tells the story of many who have 'gone overboard' on mystical or spiritual experiences, from the Montanists, through the Anabaptists to the 'French Prophets' at the time of Wesley and modern 'charismatics' of different types . . . the list is endless, and all such have needed to hold a firm grasp on the creeds and the central doctrines of the faith, to stop them from drifting off into 'heresy' or something definitely outside historic Christianity.

On the other hand the church has always faced the temptation of becoming fossilized in the security of its creeds and doctrinal traditions – and thus of losing the excitement and vitality of a living experience of Christ through the Spirit. At such periods and places, worship becomes dull and routine, children become alienated, and the church becomes irrelevant to society around.

The answer to both dangers is to allow the pole between experience and tradition to become a triangle, with scripture at the third corner. For the Bible keeps challenging the church to rethink its doctrinal traditions, and keeps urging the church to a deeper obedience and experience of Christ. And this process will work individually, as well. The key to growth in faith, both intellectually and spiritually, is a closer relationship with the scriptures. That is Luke's message for us today!

★　　★　　★

The Fourth Sunday of Easter

Acts 4:5–12
Psalm 23
1 John 3:16–24
John 10:11–18

THE Psalm and the Gospel go closely together today: for Christians, the Shepherd who leads and feeds us through life's peaceful or dangerous terrain is our Lord Jesus Christ, the Good Shepherd who is willing even to die for his flock. At the heart of this beautiful and famous passage from John's Gospel is the statement, 'I know my own and my own know me' (v. 14); that is, the Good Shepherd has such a relationship of mutual intimacy and love with his flock that he would rather sacrifice his own life than abandon them like the 'hired hand' who runs away.

In the background to this passage lies Ezekiel 34, where the Lord promises that he himself will come to 'shepherd' his people Israel, searching for the lost, gathering them into one, and tending them in good pasture – again, in contrast to false shepherds (the leaders of Israel) who have fed off the flock instead of feeding them. In John 10 Jesus presents himself as the fulfilment of this vision of loving commitment.

1 John 3:16–24 gives us a 'sheep's-eye' view of all this. The image of the flock is not used there, but the relationship pictured between Christ and us, his children, is just the same. It all rests upon his death for us, which is the measure of the love that rings and echoes into our lives, infiltrating our hearts and motives, filling the dead corners and rising until every part of us is soaked. His is the example (v. 16a) which inspires our motivation towards each other (v. 16b), transforming our reactions to the needs of others (v. 17), and our practical responses (v. 18). And when we notice this transformation in ourselves, we receive confirmation that we really are 'of the truth' (v. 19) – that faith is not a delusion.

This remarkable passage then focuses on this issue of assurance (a prominent theme in 1 John). For many Christians faith is often an uncertain thing, accompanied by much doubt. And John says nothing here to address the intellectual doubts that often accompany faith. In fact, such questionings are part and parcel of faith in a world distracted and alienated from its Creator. No: John's concern is to set real faith (including its questionings) into the context of the relationship with God which is our essential calling as human beings.

Verse 21 gives us the key picture: a relationship in which 'our hearts do not condemn us' – that is, in which there is nothing of which we feel ashamed, nothing to keep secret, but only complete openness, full sharing, total exposure, and deep love. Imagine two people who know each other deeply, and intimately. Nothing can threaten their commitment to each other. Neither holds any surprises for the other. Each loves the other unconditionally, and with great delight. Both belong, wholly, within that relationship.

Few marriages reach this level of 'boldness', which is the word John uses to describe this quality (v. 21). The Greek word has no exact equivalent in English – it combines openness, confidence and freedom to say anything; and this 'boldness' grows in our relationship with God when not only do we have complete confidence in him, but he can have complete confidence in us that we will love his Son and one another (v. 23).

To develop such a relationship with God is the supreme goal of the spiritual life. We cannot aim higher.

★   ★   ★

The Fifth Sunday of Easter

Acts 8:26–40
Psalm 22:25–31
1 John 4:7–21
John 15:1–8

P HILIP gives us an illustration of what it means to 'abide in the
vine' – although what happened to him is certainly unusual!
Because of his sensitivity to the leading of the Holy Spirit within
him, Philip bumps into the Ethiopian minister at just the moment
when he is ready to respond to the gospel. And because Jesus's
words abide in him (John 15:7) – which includes finding Jesus in
Old Testament passages like Isaiah 53, the passage about which
the Ethiopian asks – Philip is ready to answer his question with
testimony about Jesus. The result is that Philip bears fruit and
confirms his discipleship of Jesus Christ (John 15:4, 8).

Psychiatrists tells us that, as human beings, we have three fundamental needs: of affection (the need to be loved), of affirmation
(the need to be needed) and of achievement (the need to be
successful). We can see all three reflected in today's readings, which
point to the way in which these needs are met in Christ.

The need for achievement, and success, can become a dominating,
obsessive force that drives people into ill health, ruins marriages
and wrecks families. Underneath such drivenness lies the fear of
failure. But for those who 'abide' in Christ – live their lives in
fellowship with him – 'fruitfulness' is assured. It may not be dramatic conversions of others, as in Philip's case. In fact probably
another kind of 'fruit' altogether is chiefly in mind in John 15:
the fruit of love. In a world so desperately in need of it, to be a
centre and source of genuine love is achievement indeed. 'Apart
from me you can do nothing' (John 15:5). Real achievement, fruit
that lasts (15:16), is only possible through Jesus Christ.

The need to be needed? John 15 subtly underlines how significant
we are to God. Like a gardener he tends us, so that we will bear

fruit for him (v. 2), and thus bring 'glory' to him (v. 8). It's a marvellous picture of God lavishing 100% care on nurturing us, so as to win first prize at the heavenly Fruit and Veg Show! We gain much from being needed by fellow human beings – but what about being needed by God?

And the need for love? 1 John 4 is one of the most powerful passages on love in the whole New Testament, ranking alongside 1 Corinthians 13, although very different. John describes its basis and origin in the love of God shown in Christ through his death for us (vv. 7–10). Then he describes its implantation into us, through the gift of the Spirit, and by the baptismal confession, so that God himself comes to 'live' in us, turning the external expression of his love on the cross into an internal principle within us (vv. 11–16).

Next he outlines the greatest consequence of this gift: the banishing of all fear, both fear of God (v. 17) and fear of others (v. 18). And finally he underlines its practical expression in love for one another (vv. 19–21). With devastating logic, he points out that a failure to love our brothers and sisters in Christ makes a total mockery of our Christianity.

Yes, we need to abide in Christ.

★   ★   ★

The Sixth Sunday of Easter

Acts 10:44–48
Psalm 98
1 John 5:1–6
John 15:9–17

WE continue our readings in John 15 and in the First Letter of John, and again the readings are parallel in theme. Both connect loving God with loving each other: as 1 John 5:1 puts it pithily, 'Everyone who loves the father loves his child.' Our love for each other is thus an index of the strength of our love for God. And both connect loving God with obeying his commands. They are even identified in 1 John 5:3: 'This is love for God, to obey his commands.' Jesus applies the same thought to the relationship with himself in John 15:14, 'You are my friends (my loved ones) if you do what I command.'

But this is not so easy to understand. For how can love be commanded? This is not possible within human relationships. Love must be won, and cannot be extracted by edict. And friendship dies if one partner starts to issue orders to the other. Friendship grows out of mutuality, and sharing, not authority.

The answer in part, of course, is that we are dealing with God here. He does have a certain right to call the shots! But that is not the whole answer. Further reflection takes us to the heart of the Christian understanding of 'law'. Does Christianity mean living by certain rules of conduct, which typify Christian life in the same way as the fundamental laws of Islam and Buddhism shape everyday life for Muslims and Buddhists?

The importance given by Jesus to the Ten Commandments (e.g. Mark 10:17–19) suggests that the answer is 'Yes'. But John helps us to dig deeper. For he shows Jesus calling his disciples 'friends' rather than 'servants' (John 15:14–15). 'Servants' are those who simply receive a command, and obey it. 'Friends' enjoy an altogether different relationship.

Why then all this talk of obeying commands, expressed even as if obedience were a condition of continued friendship: 'If you obey my commands, you will remain in my love' (John 15:10)? The answer is that these 'commands' are not rules of conduct, in the sense of the laws by which Christian life is lived, but they are the constraints of the relationship into which we have entered with God and with his Son.

Every relationship exerts constraints. They are summarized in the marriage service by the vows the couple take. These vows then become, not commandments imposed by an outside authority, but the tracks on which their marriage runs, the air that bears these love-birds aloft, the soil out of which their relationship will feed and grow. Jesus's 'commands' are like this.

This is why 'his commands are not burdensome' (1 John 5:3): once you are in love, it's not difficult to do what the relationship demands!

Not difficult . . . but possibly very challenging and costly. Peter found it so, the day he went to Cornelius's house to speak about Jesus. He found that the Holy Spirit had got there first. And so for the first time in his life, Peter had to suppress his scruples and enter a Gentile home, to eat and sleep there. Love demanded no less. For he who loves the parent loves the child, and the lovers of God must be wherever he is, and love with his heart.

★   ★   ★

Ascension Day

Acts 1:1–11 *or* Daniel 7:9–14
Psalm 47 *or* Psalm 93
Ephesians 1:15–23 *or* Acts 1:1–11
Luke 24:44–53

ASCENSION Day, more than any other point in the Calendar, determines our world-view as Christians – that is, our sense of what truly makes our world tick, of the fundamental things that we want to say about it. Is its history meaningless, a random succession of disordered events? Is its suffering purposeless? Are human beings helpless victims of powers beyond their control – the forces of nature, politics, world markets, racial division, even of their own psychological make-up? People seem helpless before all these powers, but on Ascension Day Christians take upon themselves the dramatic confession that Jesus is Lord, so that ultimate power rests in his hands.

But Ascension Day is rather hidden in the Calendar. It does not fall on a Sunday, and receives little prominence. This is a symbol of the way we believe Christ exercises his power. No display or compulsion, but a quiet healing of bruised reeds and smouldering wicks (Matthew 12:20).

Even the story of the Ascension remains obscure. Luke deliberately combines two traditions about it – presumably both were current in his day. According to one, represented in his Gospel, Jesus ascended on the evening of Easter Day (Luke 24:50–51). According to the other, represented in Acts 1 (also by Luke), Jesus ascended at the end of a forty-day period during which he appeared frequently to his disciples (v. 3). By including both, Luke gives us the impression that he believed the Ascension was not a single event, but a period of time during which Jesus was passing between earth and heaven, reappearing often to speak to his disciples before finally being taken from them.

It is interesting that Luke picks out the issues of kingdom and of time from their conversations. 'Lord, is this the time when you will restore the kingdom to Israel?' (Acts 1.6). Like the disciples, we too long for a world set to rights, in which 'kingdom' is exercised by powers that do not crush the innocent and reward the wicked. The disciples are beginning to realize that Jesus has a pivotal role in bringing this about: will you do it, now, Lord? Jesus's reply points to an ultimate transformation, but emphasizes the meantime: he will exercise 'power' by giving his Spirit to the church, and sending us out as witnesses to him (vv. 7–8).

What must the witnesses say? In part, we confess precisely that Jesus is the ascended Lord. The lectionary provides Daniel 7 and Ephesians 1 as alternative readings, either of which points us to our testimony. Daniel wrote to enable Israel to face and endure dreadful oppression by a fearful foreign power. He receives a vision of the throne of God, before which dominion, power and authority are given to one of God's choosing, called 'a son of man', and the ugly 'beast' representing oppressive imperial power is destroyed. The New Testament frequently identifies Jesus as this 'son of man'.

Similarly Ephesians came to a small Christian group surrounded by powerful occult and pagan forces in first-century Ephesus. The great Temple of Diana symbolized the rampant powers of evil in their world. But the author urges them to see Christ, raised above all powers, seated at God's side and ruling as 'head over all things for the church' (Ephesians 1:22).

In a lost and suffering world, that's today's confession.

★   ★   ★

The Seventh Sunday of Easter
Sunday after Ascension Day

Acts 1:15–17, 21–26
Psalm 1
1 John 5:9–13
John 17:6–19

'GEARING up for mission' is a suitable slogan to attach to this Sunday, sitting between Ascension and Pentecost. We are in the interim period, when the disciples are waiting in Jerusalem for the promised Holy Spirit, who will empower them for their task (Luke 24:49).

That is not, of course, the actual setting of today's Gospel. We go back in time, and listen to Jesus praying for the disciples on the eve of his crucifixion. But 'gearing up for mission' well describes the thrust of his prayer, and the other readings gather around this focus as well.

'As you sent me into the world, I have sent them into the world' (John 17:18). These words in Jesus's prayer are terrifying! We could try to shuffle out of their challenge, by arguing that they only apply to the first disciples. But that won't work. John certainly believed that Jesus was giving a kind of charter for the whole church in this prayer. But how can we possibly carry on Jesus's mission to the world? People generally have two doubts about their capacity for it:

80

- How can we understand Jesus well enough to be able to represent him rightly?
- And how can we cope with the opposition we might experience?

Our readings address these two anxieties.

(1) Understanding Jesus. 'I gave them the words you gave me,' Jesus says (John 17:8), and these are the words they must take to the world. Certainly, we need to be well instructed in the basics of our faith, if we are going to talk about it intelligently.

But what exactly do we need to know? This is summarized in 1 John 5 as 'the testimony', or more exactly 'God's testimony, which he has given about his Son' (v. 9). The content of this 'testimony' is given in verse 8 as 'the Spirit, the water, and the blood', which is a vivid way of focusing the story of Jesus's life around its key events: his baptism, at which the Spirit descended upon him as he rose from the water, and his death, the shedding of his blood on our behalf. The Spirit came to empower him for the life of ministry that fell between these two events, and in both his baptism and his death he identified himself with the sinners he came to save.

That's it, in a nutshell! The story of Jesus, his sharing and bearing of our sin. It's interesting that, when the disciples came to replace Judas (our Acts reading), the essential qualification for his successor was that he should have been present all through the story, 'beginning from John's baptism to the time when Jesus was taken up from us' (Acts 1:22). And John adds that this 'testimony' becomes part of us, in our hearts (v. 10), because we too receive the Spirit, are baptized, know the forgiveness of sins, and experience eternal life in Christ (v. 11).

(2) Facing opposition. Yes, Jesus makes it sound tough. But he prays for the protection of his disciples (John 17:11, 15). Who knows what we may face? But through the cross comes resurrection, for all who walk in the footsteps of Jesus Christ.

And so we prepare ourselves for that absolute essential, without which all mission is doomed to failure – the gift of the Holy Spirit. Pentecost awaits.

★   ★   ★

Day of Pentecost
(Whit Sunday)

Acts 2:1–21 *or* Ezekiel 37:1–14
Psalm 104:24–34, 35b
Romans 8:22–27 *or* Acts 2:1–21
John 15:26–27; 16:4b–15

I N churches all over the world, on this day, someone draws the short straw and has to struggle with the list of countries and peoples represented in that bewildered Pentecost crowd (Acts 2:9–11). Why does Luke compile this list? Do we really need to know where they all came from? Could we omit the list without harming the story?

This question isn't silly. It actually reveals something profound about Pentecost. In recent years, in many parts of the church, the Holy Spirit has been 'rediscovered' as the living power of God, present now to inspire worship, increase love and maybe even give 'supernatural' gifts like the speaking in tongues that marked the first Pentecost. In this tradition, speaking in tongues is experienced as an intensely personal welling up of worship, finding expression in a flow of language unknown to the speaker. The emphasis falls on the Spirit as the enabler of the church – allowing the church to be itself, the Body of Christ, equipped with gifts of ministry and with power.

There is much that the church at large should learn from this tradition! But this emphasis bypasses a vital feature of the Pentecost story, which is brought out also in our Gospel from John 16. Some New Testament scholars have pointed out that Luke makes Pentecost the counterpart to the curse of Babel. In that story in Genesis 11:1–9, God confuses the speech of humankind, so that people are scattered across the earth and cannot build a magnificent city in opposition to God. As a result, the nations are born. But now a group is gathered from the nations, and hears about 'the wonders of God' (Acts 2:11) in a single language which repairs the damage done by the curse of Babel. God is ready to let humankind rediscover its fundamental unity – in Christ.

But there is more to it than this. That crowd was already united – all Jews or proselytes, gathered in Jerusalem for the Jewish festival of Pentecost, and already able to communicate through Greek, the universal language of the eastern Mediterranean (in which Peter preaches). The point is – they hear the gospel message in their own dialects, the language of 'back home', relevant therefore to all their people, whether Jews or Greek-speakers or not.

The Spirit inspires a message for the world, rather than for the church. And this is to be his distinctive ministry, according to John 16:8–11. He comes to convict the world of sin, righteousness and judgment – in other words, to convince the world that these things must all be defined around Jesus:

- the greatest sin is not to believe in him;
- though a crucified criminal he above all is 'righteous', vindicated before God; and
- his cross is actually the moment and place at which the powers of evil have been defeated.

The church already believes this! But 'the world' does not. And the Spirit comes to put that right. So Pentecost is primarily about mission – the co-operative mission of the church and the Spirit. 'He will testify about me, and you also must testify' (John 15:26f.). It is certainly right for Christians to seek the gift of the Spirit; but if he comes, he will make us missionaries.

★   ★   ★

Trinity Sunday
(Sunday after Pentecost)

Isaiah 6:1–8
Psalm 29
Romans 8:12–17
John 3:1–17

I T is certainly appropriate that, once a year, we should reflect on the Trinity, that most fundamental doctrine of our faith: that our God is three Persons in one, united in 'substance', but distinct in 'nature', yet one God, not three. This doctrine, of course, was shaped by the early church, using language not found in the Bible. Its technical terms, like 'person', 'substance' and 'nature', do not appear in the Bible in connection with the relationship between Father, Son and Holy Spirit.

So a vital focus of our reflection must be: do we find anything like this doctrine in scripture, albeit expressed differently? And can we see from scripture why the early church felt impelled towards it? These are big questions, but let us fire them at today's readings.

Isaiah 6:1–8 describes Isaiah's magnificent vision of 'the King, the Lord Almighty' in the Temple. In itself this prompts no thoughts towards 'three persons in one God', until we encounter John's quotation of this passage (John 12:39–41). John makes it a vision of Jesus's glory. Why? Because John works from the presupposition that 'no one has ever seen God' and that only the Son has 'made him known' (John 1:18). So Isaiah cannot have seen God himself. This looks like special pleading on John's part, but we need to bear in mind that 'no one can see God and live' is the usual message of the Old Testament. John is trying to rescue the Old Testament from inconsistency. So for him a vision of God becomes a vision of Jesus, and this fits with his view that the glory displayed by Jesus is the glory of God himself (John 1:14).

Our Gospel reading from John 3 prompts different reflections, but they lead in a similar direction. Jesus tells Nicodemus that he cannot 'see' or 'enter' the kingdom of God without being 'born from above'. This 'birth from above' is then ascribed to the activity of the Holy Spirit, and linked to faith in Jesus. We can sense the dramatic force of this when we realize that every Jew expected to 'enter' the kingdom of God. As 'the teacher of Israel' (v. 10), Nicodemus would never have doubted his place in the kingdom. But now entry to God's kingdom is conditional on faith in Jesus, and apparently the Spirit of God gives this special 'birth' to everyone who believes in Jesus.

Why did the first Christians start to say such things about Jesus? Our Romans 8 reading gives us some clues. It would be more helpful, in fact, if the reading began at verse 9 rather than verse 12, for verses 9–10 reveal a remarkable fluidity of language about the Holy Spirit. He is the Spirit of God, but also the Spirit of Christ (v. 9). And having 'the Spirit of Christ' is equivalent to having Christ, apparently (v. 10).

The reason for this amazing language is simply that Paul, like all the first Christians, was convinced that Jesus had won salvation for the church, and that at the heart of this salvation was the gift of the Holy Spirit (vv. 13–16). If Jesus is the giver of the Spirit of God, then clearly he must enjoy an absolutely unique relationship with God himself.

The doctrine of the Trinity? Moving in that direction!

★ ★ ★

The Sundays after Trinity

Proper 4
(Sunday between 29 May and 4 June)

1 Samuel 3:1–10 *or* 1 Samuel 3:1–20 *with* Psalm 139:1–6, 13–18
or Deuteronomy 5:12–15 *with* Psalm 81:1–10
2 Corinthians 4:5–12
Mark 2:23–3:6

THE gem of a tale told in 1 Samuel 3 of the boy Samuel's first experience of his vocation as a prophet is not just a story about God's call; it is also an episode in a nation's relationship with their God. Just as Samuel is a young boy, and impressionable, so too the nation is young and led astray by second-rate leaders. Samuel's openness to the dictates of conscience and goodness contrasts with the self-seeking and immorality of Eli's sons. He is open to guidance, whereas they are only fit for judgment. Nevertheless, we should note Eli's wisdom and readiness to bear whatever God disposes.

Psalm 139 celebrates such a God, who knows in graciousness, not in judgment, and who cares and loves and expends himself in compassion. There is nowhere the Psalmist might go, but that God will be with him and guide his every move. For some, such a relationship with the divine might be thought too claustrophobic; here it is experienced as life-giving and enabling.

Deuteronomy reiterates the commandment from Exodus 20:8 and roots it in the saving events of Israel's history. The sabbath is to be kept because the nation was subject to slavery; presumably with no day of rest. So there is a typological link maintained with the details of Israel's past.

Psalm 81 makes the same point, though the commandment referred to is different; and the giving of the Law was consequent upon God's rescue of the people out of slavery. His moral demand upon them was based upon his graciousness in releasing them from oppression.

Paul in 2 Corinthians is working through his argument in justification of his apostleship and ministry. In today's passage he reaches one of his sublimest moments – and one where he is frequently misunderstood. He alludes to the story of creation in Genesis 1:3, 'Then God said, "Let there be light".' These two small words in Hebrew are part of the dynamic of the passage which is moving towards the creation of humankind, in God's image, and that is the main point of the passage. Paul's assertion, 'For it is the God who said, "Let light shine out of darkness," who has shone in our hearts to give the light of the knowledge of the glory of God in the face of Jesus Christ,' has a twofold effect. First, it places Christ within the context of creation and makes him a second Adam; second, it associates believers with Christ, making them also part of the wonder of creation.

Paul continues with the image of 'things made of clay'. The expression 'clay jars' suggests that the image is one of vessels which 'contain' the gospel. However, the Greek word is of much wider meaning than that: the reference throughout the passage is one of change; even of transfiguration. What Paul is saying is that we who are believers, we who preach the gospel, are like things made of clay, which are constantly and repeatedly being changed from dust into glory. That is why he is able to say, 'We are afflicted in every way, but not crushed; perplexed, but not driven to despair; persecuted, but not forsaken; struck down, but not destroyed; always carrying in the body the death of Jesus, so that the life of Jesus may also be made visible in our bodies.'

The Gospel, taking up again the continuous reading of Mark, has Jesus making the shocking assertion that the Law was written for the well-being of humanity; the kind of adherence to Law which simply asserts that it must be obeyed without regard for its human consequences is therefore empty and inhuman legalism.

★　　★　　★

Proper 5

(Sunday between 5 and 11 June)

1 Samuel 8:4–11, 16–20 *or* 1 Samuel 8:4–20 *or* 1 Samuel 8:4–20
and 1 Samuel 11:14–15 *with* Psalm 138
or Genesis 3:8–15 *with* Psalm 130
2 Corinthians 4:13–5:1
Mark 3:20–35

T HE readings in Track 1 betray the biblical ambivalence about
kingship. There were perhaps originally differing traditions;
if so, they have been combined in the final text so that both sit
alongside one another. The unsatisfactory characters of Samuel's
sons leads the people to desire an alternative system – but one
which will be detrimental both to the relationship with God and
to the well-being of the nation. All the disadvantages are spelled
out, and the people are left in no doubt that they will be worse
off with a king than without.

In this context Psalm 138 is a reminder, on the lips of the people
of Israel, that God is the protector of his people, and that they
may trust in his goodness to guide and direct them. However this
is no passive care; rather, God's acts of the past are recalled, and
he is called upon to 'stretch forth [his] hand against the fury' of
oppressors and save by his 'right hand'.

The (Track 2) reading from Genesis tells of the aftermath of what
we have come to regard as 'The Fall'. In reality, however, the
whole episode rehearses the ambiguities of human responsibility.
Here we have Adam's fear and his attempt to shift responsibility
on to his wife for what happened. When God came looking for
Adam that evening, he had the chance, not just to own up to
what he had done, but even to assert his humanity and freedom,
and thus remake the relationship. But he missed it, and simply
started the cycle of blame. Knowledge of good and evil is necessary
and wonderful, but it has consequences which are very mixed.

The Psalm takes up the theme of the declaration of guilt. Nevertheless, 'there is forgiveness with God', and the wise soul waits and expects deliverance from the oppression of guilt. The Psalm is based upon the conviction that God's business is forgiveness. The sense of pardon may take a while coming, but its guarantee is sure, for it is rooted in the character of God.

From the theme of suffering for sin we move with Paul's Second Letter to Corinth to suffering for the sake of proclaiming the gospel. Again, however, the outcome is certain, for the present, 'slight, momentary affliction is preparing us for an eternal weight of glory beyond all measure'.

The continuing reading from Mark's Gospel tells of another field of conflict, that of domestic relationships. There is some comfort here to the normal family to recognize that the household in which Jesus was brought up also had its tensions. It is salutary to note that the tensions are brought about by the son's insistence upon the priority of his vocation above family ties. This is a difficult issue, for the tradition we share with Judaism calls upon human beings to honour their father and mother, and we have a story of Jesus criticizing those who skirted their responsibilities to their parents by means of religious gifts and observance (cf. Mark 7:11). Nevertheless here is a lesson to the churches today, which often collude with an uncritical idolatry of 'the family', forgetting that the primary family, for Christian people, is the human race, and the honour that is due to parents is due to all people. The family is the primary testing ground for the values of the kingdom of God; when it takes over from the kingdom's demands, then it has overstepped its boundaries.

★   ★   ★

Proper 6
(Sunday between 12 and 18 June)

1 Samuel 15:34–16:13 *with* Psalm 20
or Ezekiel 17:22–24 *with* Psalm 92:1–4, 12–15
2 Corinthians 5:6–10, 14–17 *or* 2 Corinthians 5:6–17
Mark 4:26–34

ANOTHER powerful story brings to an effective end the ambi-valent tradition concerning kingship as it focused in Saul. Samuel is chided by God for grieving over Saul and told to go and anoint one of Jesse's sons to succeed him. Jesse's sons pass before Samuel and, not surprisingly in tales of this nature, it is the youngest and least likely who is the chosen one – 'for the Lord looks not on the outward appearance, but on the heart' (1 Samuel 16:6).

Psalm 20 is a royal Psalm, a prayer for the king. The Psalmist is confident that 'the name of the Lord our God' is more powerful than chariots and horses.

The Ezekiel passage is a metaphor for God's power over history. The cedar sprig symbolizes Israel planted on the mountain of Zion; the nations of the earth recognize God's superiority, for he raises up and brings low, he punishes and he rehabilitates, and Israel's recent history has demonstrated that.

Psalm 92 is a hymn of praise, for singing on the sabbath, for the continuing, reliable 'loving-kindness' of God. Instruments of music are to be used to sing God's praise as the 'righteous' – those who have and keep God's Law – expect to reach a ripe and fruitful old age. When the Psalmist calls God 'my rock', he is acknowledging his faith in God's complete dependability.

Reading 2 Corinthians 5, one wonders whether this is evidence on Paul's part of a desire to die, as in Philippians 1:23, where he speaks of his desire 'to depart and be with Christ, which is far better'. Here, as there, however, he is constrained to preach the gospel, so he has no alternative. Having thus considered this possibility – and desirability – he realizes that he has looked death or derangement in the face and reckons that he can no longer view people 'from [such a] a human point of view' – that is, in terms of his own wants and preferences. He is committed to the Corinthians and rediscovers his love for them. So a fundamental conviction is strengthened: in Christ there is a 'new creation', which takes control over the past, with all its personal and self-centred ambitions – even the desire for death.

Mark 4 tells another parable of the kingdom of God. The seed grows secretly, but certainly, until the harvest, when the sickle will be put in to cut the corn; this is a symbol of judgment. The parable of the mustard seed contrasts the beginning with the end; the meaning of both of these parables is left to the hearers' and readers' interpretations. The secret is revealed in the mystery and in the contrast; in the judgment there will be an end to scarcity, to meanness and to ignorance.

★ ★ ★

Proper 7
(Sunday between 19 and 25 June)

1 Samuel 17:(1a, 4–11, 19–23), 32–49 *with* Psalm 9:9–20
or 1 Samuel 17:57–18:5, 10–16 *with* Psalm 133
or Job 38:1–11 *with* Psalm 107:1–3, 23–32
2 Corinthians 6:1–13
Mark 4:35–41

THE story of David and Goliath is one of the classics; it establishes David's reputation as a godly and gifted figure, eager to defend the nation of Israel against attack. The power of the Philistine is apparently overwhelming, the potential ruin the Israelites face is unbearable, and the chances of escape for the nation from this threat seem unlikely in the extreme. But David knows what he has to do; he is a faithful and courageous Israelite, who has experience of defending his flocks from wild animals. He therefore uses what skills he has in the service of his God; the only difference is that the odds against which he is pitched are rather greater than those to which he is accustomed. Many times he would have used his small sling to cast stones against marauding beasts; now his enemy is the enemy of his people, not just his flock, and this beast is as doomed as any lion or bear.

David's plan is successful; he so angers his opponent that the giant of a man is insulted by the implication that a mere lad might be considered his equal in battle. David takes advantage of his discomfiture, takes aim and pitches the pebble. He believes, however, that what he is doing is fighting in the name of the Lord his God, so the weapons are immaterial; as far as he is concerned, God will deliver this man into his hand. And so he does.

Psalm 9 reflects this sense that it is God who fights for the under-dog; those who put their trust in him will not be disappointed. The Psalmist prays for protection in the confidence that he will not be let down.

The alternative reading tells the story of what happened after David's amazing victory; Saul was so impressed with his prowess on the battlefield that he made him commander over his army. Unfortunately David's very success began to turn Saul's mind, and he became jealous of him. Nevertheless David's fame was assured, and God ensured that his success continued.

Psalm 133 is almost ironical, in view of Saul's attitude to David, when read in the light of the lesson. The two of them did not live in unity, even if the people were unified under David's military prowess.

The Track 2 reading from Job is the beginning of God's response to Job after all his complaints. God has given Job a horrible time, and Job's friends have come and 'comforted' him – if that is the right word. Their various observations on his plight boiled down to the view that Job must have earned God's displeasure in some way for all those things to have happened to him which are related in Job 1. Job has maintained his innocence throughout his ordeal, and his comforters have not been able to get him to see his 'folly'.

Now God himself responds to all that has been said and, in a grossly imbalanced show of strength, asserts his authority over Job, over his friends and, indeed, over all creation. Job had never claimed to have the Creator's control over all things, but now he is judged as if he had made just such a blasphemous claim. Still Job is the object of God's unpleasantness.

Paul was better placed to turn his misfortunes to good theological effect; he could at least see the results of his trials in the lives of the communities that he had founded. His commitment was to preaching the good news of Jesus Christ, and to establishing communities of people who were committed in faith to him. This may have resulted in all kinds of injury, indignity and insult, but his faith remained firm – at least in retrospect! In the end, he has no doubt, there will be glorious vindication in the resurrection of all people from the dead. And even now, he knows in advance, by the Spirit, the reality of that belief.

Mark's Gospel continues with Jesus leaving the house of confrontation with his mother and brothers and going across the lake of Galilee. A great storm arises, and the disciples fear for their lives. Jesus, asleep on a cushion in the boat throughout all this, is surprised to be woken: 'Storm? What storm?' And he calms it with the words, 'Peace! Be still!' This is not simply a little miracle to calm the fears of his disciples – they were fishermen, after all. This is Jesus, the Son of God, asserting his authority over creation, to raise to life and to quell the watery monster of chaos – as God had done in Genesis 1. The question is rhetorical, 'Who then is this, that even the wind and the sea obey him?' The answer may be obvious to the believers who read and retell the story, but the implications are staggering.

★   ★   ★

Proper 8

(Sunday between 26 June and 2 July)

2 Samuel 1:1, 17–27 *with* Psalm 130
or Wisdom of Solomon 1:13–15; 2:23–24
with Lamentations 3:23–33 *or* Psalm 30
2 Corinthians 8:7–15
Mark 5:21–43

For all that David had suffered at the hands of Saul, he did not write him off. When Saul died, David mourned him. Here is one of the finest poetic laments in the scriptures – and all over a king who, finally, was regarded as a failure. The lament is also for Jonathan, who was David's close friend, and whose love 'pass[ed] the love of women'.

Such are the depths of sadness to which human life is prone, and from such depths the Psalmist calls to God. Psalm 130 concentrates on the guilt rather than the suffering; yet the hope for redemption is such that it will embrace both forgiveness and vindication.

The Wisdom of Solomon asserts that death is an aberration, an intervention into life; this is an interesting case of the influence of the kind of thinking which cannot see that God is, in some sense, responsible also for what is amiss in the world. It contrasts with Isaiah 45:7, 'I make weal and create woe'.

Lamentations 3:23–33 speaks of God's faithfulness and his mercies which are 'new every morning'; the lesson to be learned is that, although insults and suffering may come, they will not last for ever.

Psalm 30 is a celebration of vindication; the Psalmist has been close to death but has been restored; life and happiness have been threatened, but well-being has been restored. There is no virtue, as far as God is concerned, in death, for he is God of the living.

2 Corinthians has Paul commending the Corinthians for their excellence in all spiritual gifts; he wants them to go one stage

further and give generously in response to the gift of God in Christ. This is the collection for the church in Jerusalem which he is arranging. He invests this with theological significance, so that the Gentiles may acknowledge that their heritage is from Israel and from the Hebrew scriptures.

Mark has the story of the daughter of Jairus, the ruler of the synagogue, and the woman with the haemorrhage – both insignificant characters in society at the time, but both precious to Jesus. By the interleaving of the stories it is clear that they are intended to be read together; this is not simply to do with historicity. Both characters are female, and the older one has suffered haemorrhages for as long as the younger one has been alive – twelve years. The girl is the daughter of Jairus, and Jesus addressed the woman as a 'Daughter', as he heals her. The older woman is socially dead, because her condition makes her ritually unclean, and therefore an outcast; the girl dies in the course of the story.

Jesus's command that the parents should not tell anyone what had happened is curious; everyone knew that the girl was dead, and it would be clear what had happened. In part, this may be regarded as consistent with Mark's theological framework in which Jesus insists that his Messiahship be kept secret. But when we ask what is the function of this secrecy in the narrative, it becomes clearer that, as the reader enters the world of silence enjoined by the text, the question drills itself deeper into the mind, not simply of who Jesus is – if the answer is, in some sense, 'Messiah' – but also of what kind of Messiah he may be. By transgressing legal taboos, Jesus brings a wholeness to people which adherence to Mosaic Law can never deliver. Human societies take a long time to awaken to these gospel insights, and we are only just beginning, in the West – and that reluctantly – to explore the implications of all this.

However, we are gradually learning that a willingness to acknowledge the full humanity of those whom society – largely at the church's instigation – has branded as sexual outcasts is the only way to bear full witness to the gospel of Jesus Christ, who brings in God's reign of compassion and community for all.

★   ★   ★

Proper 9

(Sunday between 3 and 9 July)

2 Samuel 5:1–5, 9–10 *with* Psalm 48
or Ezekiel 2:1–5 *with* Psalm 123
2 Corinthians 12:2–10
Mark 6:1–13

I N the story of David's becoming king there is no trace of the
ambivalence which the earlier texts express towards the very
idea of kingship; we are left here with the sense that, in becoming
king, David is succeeding to his rightful place at the head of Israel's
affairs, and that this succession is what both the people and God
desire. His power has yet to be consolidated, however, and the
stronghold of Jerusalem holds out against him; but it will not be
long before he is able to assert his authority over all the kingdom.

Psalm 48 expresses the Psalmist's delight in the city of Zion, which
is the name of the hill upon which Jerusalem is built. The faith
of the Jewish scriptures is largely related to a sense of place, and
here its beauty, strength and status are all celebrated. What is most
significant about this city, however, is that this city is the dwelling
place of God, and that is at his own choice. The absence of any
image of him suggests that he has not been brought there, as the
gods of other cities have been to their cities; here God's name
dwells, and that means his unfathomable character.

In Track 2 the Old Testament reading prepares for the Gospel by
telling of the call of the prophet Ezekiel. Preceding this passage is
the vision he has of God's throne in heaven; now he is addressed
by a voice which, first, asserts his value as the object of God's call
and, second, tells him of the task which God has in store for him.
He is to be an emissary from God to speak to the rebellious nation
which is Israel.

Psalm 123 is chosen presumably because it reflects the obedience
which is proper from those who are to be God's agents. The
servant, male or female, who is constantly attentive to the desires

of their master or mistress is biddable by a look or a movement of the hand; such is the understanding of the prophet's role in much of the Old Testament. We might want to assert, along with the Old Testament lesson, the primacy of the human being and his or her role in the vocation to be a prophet. This will be worked out in a mutual relationship of identifying and refining the message that shall eventually be delivered.

In today's passage from 2 Corinthians Paul reveals one of the most intimate experiences of his prayer life; so much so that he is hardly sure whether he can relate to himself the experience of which he speaks. The ecstatic state he found was such that he heard things said which were heavenly, and he thought – wrongly – that such an experience was the basis upon which he could request God for relief from a particular 'thorn in the flesh'. What he had to learn was that profound experience in prayer does not constitute any ground for escape from suffering. What he was told in response to his prayer to be relieved of pain was the simple assurance that he would be given grace to bear what was inflicted upon him.

The Gospel for today brings us back to the subject of following the call of God. First we see Jesus returning to his home town and amazing the people who know him by his capacity for teaching the things of God, apparently untutored by conventional means. He gives expression to the truth known to many, that home and family are the most difficult contexts in which to minister; too many people know too much about us. Sometimes, however, that has to be our vocation.

Second, we see the disciples being commissioned by Jesus to go out and cast out demons. Their lifestyle is to reflect their motivation and their message: the kingdom of God is imminent, and in casting out demons they are demonstrating the end of the reign of the devil. They are to take nothing for the journey; only sandals for their feet, for their work will mean that they are constantly on the move.

It is interesting to note Mark's 'matter-of-fact' tone; they simply got on and did what was required of them. We often seem to think, today, that obedience for us has to be something complicated, the subject of much agonizing. We do not literally face demons in our day, but we do have to contend with issues and circumstances which fail to embody the kingdom of God; the forces of in-humanity and intolerance are always at work in human society, and even in the church. In offering such healing to others, we do well to remember that we too stand in need of it.

★   ★   ★

Proper 10
(Sunday between 10 and 16 July)

2 Samuel 6:1–5, 12b–19 *with* Psalm 24
or Amos 7:7–15 *with* Psalm 85:8–13
Ephesians 1:3–14
Mark 6:14–29

T HE passage from 2 Samuel tells of how the ark of the Lord was brought to Jerusalem. David danced with joy on the occasion, and Michal, his wife, despised him. She was the daughter of Saul, and in happier, earlier times she had helped David to escape from the rage of her father and his murderous intentions. Now she is estranged from him and is punished by him for refusing to join in the great party, with food for all, with which he celebrates the coming of the ark to Jerusalem.

Psalm 24 is a song of ascent which pilgrims sang as they went up to Jerusalem. The great city is described as having been built upon seas and established upon floods, so there is clearly a sense in which its foundation is seen as the work of God in his creative victory over the forces of evil.

The Track 2 reading has Amos prophesying what the people do not want to hear, and getting into trouble for it. Psalm 85 speaks of telling the truth, which is fundamentally gracious, for it is coupled always with mercy. Truth is not bare and cold, for there is a moral element to it, which is engaging and which issues in forgiveness and affirmation.

Ephesians 1:3–14 starts a serial reading of this amazing Epistle. It was probably not written by Paul, but by a disciple who wanted to honour his memory after his death. Here the writer sets out the praise of God for his work in blessing and election, in redemption through Christ, and in 'sealing' – guaranteeing the position of God's people – with the Holy Spirit. This threefold schema is an early example of the Christian sense of the variety of God's presence to humanity as fundamentally one. God elects, or chooses, people, and the model for this is his choice of Israel; this is now generalized to his choice of people other than Israel. God also redeems people, and this is the particular focus of the death of Jesus, which is seen as an atoning sacrifice. He also 'seals' people with his Spirit, puts his mark upon them and makes them his own, in baptism.

John the Baptist's fate in Mark is significant, for it constitutes the impetus for the start of the public work of Jesus. John plays a remarkably large part in the Marcan narrative. It could be that his significance at the time was such that he merited this attention in any story of Jesus; it is also possible that Mark wishes to provide an appropriate context for the ministry of Jesus; another possibility is that Jesus had earlier been one of John's disciples. Now John must pay the price for his fearless proclamation of God's judgment on the behaviour of the king, Herod, who had married his brother's wife. Amos had also suffered the indignity of the rejection of his message; John pays for his courage with his life.

★   ★   ★

Proper 11

(Sunday between 17 and 23 July)

2 Samuel 7:1–14a *with* Psalm 89:20–37
or Jeremiah 23:1–6 *with* Psalm 23
Ephesians 2:11–22
Mark 6:30–34, 53–56

WHEREAS earlier narratives spoke of ambivalence about king-ship, the narratives concerning Solomon and David are every bit as ambivalent about the building of a Temple. God does not need a house; and, for all that he seems to appreciate being offered one, the message is that David himself will not be the one to build it; that will be Solomon's task. God will, however, establish David's house, that is, his dynasty.

Psalm 89 underlines the differing functions of David and Solomon, by focusing upon David's role as the head of the dynasty and the type of a faithful ruler. Just as Saul bore the ambiguity of kingship, so Solomon bears the ambiguity of Temple worship; David is left inviolate in his reputation in this respect.

The Track 2 reading from Jeremiah tells of leaders who scatter rather than gather the flock. David is known as the faithful shepherd, and this memory informs the prophecy. Psalm 23 is a fitting accompaniment to this passage, with its apparent pastoral setting which nevertheless speaks of a strength and commitment to caring for the sheep. The image soon gives way, however, to one of permanent residence in the house of God, which is where the worshipper wishes to be.

Ephesians 2 divides into two halves, both of them about reconcili-ation. The first half, not read here, focuses upon reconciliation between God and humanity; the second, here, upon reconciliation between the races of humanity. There are only Jews and Gentiles, so the whole of humanity is reconciled, both with God and within itself. However, this is not so much a theory of how reconciliation (which is the same as atonement, for the word means making 'at-one') came about; rather is it a claim that all races are one, because all races share in the action of Christ in reconciling humanity to God. They must be one, because there was one body of Christ offered, and both Jew and Gentile are included within the baptized community.

This is, in one sense, to emphasize what the readers already know; but it amounts to more than that because the reconciled human community, viewed as a building, grows into a Temple, which becomes organic as a body. Thus develops a remarkable image of stability, of growth in worship and of human mutuality. The details of this will be spelled out later in the Epistle.

The Gospel passage from Mark 6 has the disciples returning from their mission, and Jesus offering them rest. But they do not get it! At least, Jesus didn't. Is this the earliest warning of the danger of ministerial burn-out?

★ ★ ★

Proper 12
(Sunday between 24 July and 30 July)

2 Samuel 11:1–15 *with* Psalm 14
or 2 Kings 4:42–44 *with* Psalm 145:10–18
Ephesians 3:14–21
John 6:1–21

I T might be argued that God should have allowed David to build a Temple, then he would have been too busy to get out his binoculars and spy on the neighbours. This sad episode in the story of the great king of Israel serves a number of purposes. First, it highlights David's personal weakness, great king though he was; second, and paradoxically, it provides for David to have an heir, for Solomon is Bathsheba's son; third, it indicates the principle of forgiveness which is perhaps the most significant feature of the relationship between Israel and their God. David's behaviour is the lowest of the low: he sees what he wants, he determines to have it at all costs and he has a loyal subject and soldier killed. Even heroes of the faith are not complete paragons of virtue.

Psalm 14 mocks the folly of those who deny God; David's behaviour is thus set in the context of 'the human race' – not 'us all' (v. 2) by this juxtaposition; it is as though we are intended to read 'he might as well be a heathen!' Similarly, we might read Uriah the Hittite's position as the same as the people of God when they are under persecution or threat.

The Old Testament readings in Track 2 set the context for the miraculous feeding which is told in John 6. The context of this story in 2 Kings is itself instructive, for it occurs at the end of a number of stories about God's miraculous provision of food, and it precedes the healing from leprosy of Naaman the Syrian; there are tones here which clearly find their echo in the feeding stories in the Gospels, including his servant's protest at the impossibility of the task.

Psalm 145 sings the praise of God who provides food for all. The worshippers are commanded to sing God's praise, and the descriptions of what God has done are intended to arouse thanksgiving. In particular, these verses celebrate the glories of God's rule, which is exercised on behalf of those who are his people. God is celebrated as faithful, merciful and consistent in supplying all their needs.

The reading from Ephesians takes up the prayer attributed to Paul in this letter written by a disciple, probably after the apostle's death. He is depicted as desiring that the readers might be so 'lived in' by Christ, that they will come to know the limitless extent of his love. This has just been spelled out in the previous chapter, and involves making reconciliation both between humanity and God and between Jew and Gentile. In putting these words into Paul's mouth, the writer is able to draw attention to Paul's role in spreading the gospel of the reconciliation between all people and God.

The Gospel passage is, as we have noted, the miraculous feeding of the crowd of Jesus's hearers. It will become one of the great themes of the Gospel story, for 'the bread of life' has such manifold connotations. A deliberate link is made with Passover (vv. 4), and there is a subtle twist to the conversation between Jesus and his disciples as it is recorded in the Synoptic Gospels; here Jesus takes the initiative, 'for he himself knew what he was going to do'. The sign provokes the people to recognize Jesus as a prophet, but he withdraws from them to avoid their acclaiming him as king.

The incident of Jesus's walking on the water takes place in Mark's Gospel also in the context of the miraculous feeding. It underlines the themes of the presence and absence of Jesus and, in the curious detail of the timing of the disciples' wanting to take him into the boat, of the tensions between the times of their arrival at land and their sense of where they are and of how far they have travelled. These themes will be explored in John's reflections upon the significance of the bread distributed to the people.

★   ★   ★

Proper 13
(Sunday between 26 July and 6 August)

2 Samuel 11:26–12:13a *with* Psalm 51:1–12
or Exodus 16:2–4, 9–15 *with* Psalm 78:23–29
Ephesians 4:1–16
John 6:24–35

THE unedifying story of David and Bathsheba runs its course. With Uriah the Hittite dead, David allows Bathsheba an appropriate period of mourning (and we gain the impression that this is the briefest thought to be respectable) and then moves in – or rather, moves her in. It takes the prophet Nathan to point out the gross injustice of David's behaviour, by means of a parable, but David does not see the point of this until Nathan points it out to him, with his incisive, 'You are the man!' He then sets out the judgment that will befall David's house. We may think that David's penitence was a little peremptory; we may also think it a little unfair that the sins of the father are thus to be visited upon his descendants, but such were the contemporary assumptions of guilt.

Psalm 51, as most Bibles indicate, is traditionally associated with David's relationship with Bathsheba. The Psalmist is conscious of his sin; but 'against you, you only, have I sinned' is not strictly accurate: for David sinned against Uriah and Bathsheba too.

The Track 2 readings take up the theme of bread from heaven, in readiness for the discourse of Jesus upon the bread of life. Provision of food is made in response to the people's complaining about their lot; they quickly forgot how ill they were treated in Egypt! In order to satisfy them God sends food for them like dew, which is to be collected each morning.

In the light of this story Psalm 78 presents an outline of the history of God's saving acts as a hymn of praise to God. The particular section which is read today deals with God's provision of food and care for his people.

Ephesians 4 begins a section of ethical teaching based upon the theology of worship and thanksgiving that has been set out in Ephesians 1–2. The readers are urged to 'walk' (that is the meaning of the Greek word) in various ways, which develop from one another. The first, here, is 'worthy of the calling to which [they] have been called', namely, to unity. Psalm 68 plays a part in this as it is read in the light of the resurrection and exaltation of Jesus to heaven and the giving of gifts to humankind. The Hebrew text of this Psalm speaks of 'receiving gifts from men', but it is likely that this is to be understood as receiving gifts in order to redistribute them. The gifts which are given to the church take the form of people who bear office in it. Their primary purpose is 'to equip the saints for the work of ministry, for building up the body of Christ', and their ultimate aim the 'unity of the faith and of the knowledge of the Son of God'.

John 6 continues reflection upon the bread of life. Here, bread must be worked for, and that means continuing the work of Jesus. Moses is held out as the type of provider of the 'bread of heaven';

he is superseded by Jesus, who is the true bread which God gives
to those who obey him.

★   ★   ★

Proper 14
(Sunday between 7 August and 13 August)

2 Samuel 18:5–9, 15, 31–33 *with* Psalm 130
or 1 Kings 19:4–8 *with* Psalm 34:1–8
Ephesians 4:25–5:2
John 6:35, 41–51

T HE Second Book of Samuel tells of the coming of the sword
to the house of David, as had been promised, when Absalom,
David's son who rebelled against him, is killed against the wishes
of his father expressed to his officers. Not surprisingly, even in
spite of his rebellion, Absalom's death affects David deeply, and
his grief is eloquently set out as he wishes that he himself might
have died instead of his son.

Psalm 130, to be read with this passage, continues this mood, but
with the element of hope added for the resolution of grief. To
some this might sound a little premature; there is no consoling a
parent for the death of a child. Only when the parent is ready can
he or she begin to take up again the threads of living.

After his victory over the priests of Baal, Elijah is in need of
sustenance; this story is certainly about the provision made by God
for his servant, but it reflects the everyday reality that those who
serve God often find themselves to be, as it appears, inordinately
tired after some particular event or incident. Their physical needs
must be met; but this also serves as a reminder that they must also
take responsibility for ensuring that they are fed spiritually too;
this is the theme that will be taken up again in the Gospel passage.

Psalm 34 is a Psalm of thanksgiving which praises God for his

105

goodness. A sense of gratitude is what makes possible the continual 'looking upon him', so that his radiance is reflected in our lives; tasting and seeing that the Lord is good may be a very physical matter, as we give thanks for the material benefits we enjoy. They also symbolize the invitation to ensure that our spirits are nourished.

Ephesians continues its moral exhortation with what it means to walk 'no longer as the Gentiles' (Ephesians 4:17), that is, as those who remain estranged from God. As the list of virtues is developed, so we are led to a recognition that we are called to walk 'in love'.

The Gospel maintains its reflection on bread, this time with the great proclamation about the bread of life, and the rejection of this insight by 'the Jews'. They are depicted as obtuse in their rejection of Jesus and his message – and therefore of their own scriptures and tradition. Their complaint about and against him matches the complaint which their forbears made against God, when he provided the manna for them; history, evidently, is repeating itself.

Naturally we need to be wary, in our day, of demonizing Jews – as well as other ethnic and religious groups. The context of John's Gospel was one of rejection from the synagogue and denial of a common heritage. This explains why the early Christian community attacked Jews with such rigour; such traditions must not be used as a basis for discrimination today.

★   ★   ★

Proper 15
(Sunday between 14 and 20 August)

1 Kings 2:10–12; 3:3–14 *with* Psalm 111
or Proverbs 9:1–6 *with* Psalm 34:9–14
Ephesians 5:15–20
John 6:51–58

ANOTHER reading from John 6, the penultimate before the lectionary reverts to Mark's Gospel, concludes the exposition of the story of the manna in the wilderness and brings it to a climax. The discourse is built on words from Psalm 78: 'he gave them bread from heaven to eat', and the message is that whereas the manna was merely for physical sustenance in the desert, Jesus supplies the means of eternal life. Jewish interpretation of the manna had already described it in terms of Wisdom and Law and John picks this up. He is aware that the divine gift of the Bread of Life has its ceremonial enactment in the Christian Eucharist and here makes this explicit in a quite shocking way. Flesh and blood denote the real humanity of Jesus – who is to be taken and assimilated by the believer. This is not some kind of 'magic', but an intimate relationship of mutual indwelling – a personal and ethical relationship which will be elaborated in the 'true vine' imagery of chapter 15. On the eve of the Passion it will be underlined again that the Christ who really lived and really died is to be received as the revelation of the Father.

Wisdom's invitation is for drink as well as food. The related Old Testament reading is from Proverbs and presents the first part of a contrasting allegory. Wisdom has built her house and invited her guests to an inaugural banquet. Later in the same chapter 'Dame Folly' will address her invitation to the same audience. Psalm 34 makes its links with Wisdom in verses 11 and 12. The theme of the address is 'the fear of the Lord'. It starts with joy in life and expectation of future happiness and warns against doing evil.

The Old Testament reading which is set describes the death of David and the accession of King Solomon, with God's promise to him of wisdom, riches and honour. The story begins with Solomon's humility in asking for understanding and discernment from the Lord. The Psalm is a hymn of praise for God's great deeds, especially for his faithfulness to the covenant: beginning with the ritual cry 'Hallelujah' (Praise the Lord) it develops as an acrostic Psalm, every line starting with a successive letter of the Hebrew alphabet.

The Ephesians reading is one of a series of exhortations based on the image of 'walking'. It develops into a full-blown household code of which this passage is the introduction. Here carousing is contrasted with worship. To 'walk wisely' is to be filled with the spirit, and wisdom is to be found in mutual submission with a focus on prayer and holy living.

★ ★ ★

Proper 16
(Sunday between 21 and 27 August)

1 Kings 8:22–30, 41–43 *or* 1 Kings 8:1, 6, 10–11, 22–30, 41–43
with Psalm 84
or Joshua 24:1–2a, 14–18 *with* Psalm 34:15–22
Ephesians 6:10–20
John 6:56–69

THERE is something of the tying up of loose ends about today's readings. The continuous readings break and offer an opportunity for some concluding thoughts about the Deuteronomic history, Ephesians and the Fourth Gospel.

The final Johannine passage in this series brings us to the reactions of the disciples to the Bread of Life discourse and to the confession of Peter. It is not the unbelief of the Jews, this time, but of Jesus's own disciples who 'drew back' – shocked by the emphasis on 'flesh'. The usual view is that the Christian community in the background of this passage is struggling with 'docetism', a denial of the reality of Jesus's humanity and death. Peter, by contrast, makes the desired response – showing a capacity to perceive the truth by faith and personal experience. We are confronted always with a choice.

The Old Testament reading is about the dedication of the Temple – and, strangely, in Solomon's speech and prayer raises the same issue: 'Will God indeed dwell on the earth?' Psalm 84, 'How lovely is your dwelling place', makes the response of faith in a new Exodus of return through the valley, going from strength to strength in trust of Israel's God to 'withhold . . . no good thing'.

The final Ephesians passage on the whole armour of God is also something of a concluding appeal – primarily to worship as central to Christian existence. Human community is renewed in Christ. God and humanity are portrayed as reconciled. Prayer, worship and mission all come together in the call to stand firm in the spiritual battle.

The related Old Testament reading is from Joshua: the final chapter, set in Shechem, in which Joshua tells the people all that God has achieved on their behalf – and then confronts them with the choice of whether they will be faithful to the Lord or worship other gods. In the Hebrew canon the book of Joshua is included among the 'former prophets' – and the message of this passage is reminiscent of the prophets' calls to repentance and obedience. It reflects the theology of those who edited the material during the Babylonian exile: the stories demonstrate God's power, but the people must decide. Those who are faithful will be rewarded with God's blessing.

The final section of Psalm 34, set as the alternative canticle, describes true happiness as consisting in the nearness of God, and in the living experience of his help, rather than in being spared grief and suffering. It ends in praise of God who 'redeems the soul of his servants'.

★　★　★

Proper 17
(Sunday between 28 August and 3 September)

Song of Solomon 2:8–13 *with* Psalm 45:1–2, 6–9
or Deuteronomy 4:1–2, 6–9 *with* Psalm 15
James 1:17–27
Mark 7:1–8, 14–15, 21–23

TODAY marks the beginning of a five-week series of readings from the Letter of James and a return to Mark's Gospel for the remainder of this cycle. It might be an opportunity to do some sustained study of one or other of these texts. Alternatively, the Song of Songs is a much neglected treasure which deserves our attention.

First the Gospel: Mark seems to come to us from a Christian community which struggled, as Paul did, over kosher food. The hard-fought tussles attested in Acts and the Epistles would be difficult to explain if Jesus had already settled the issue. So the usual view of this controversy over ritual purity is that Jesus condemned overly narrow interpretations as frustrating the real thrust of scripture – but that this particular application, declaring all foods clean, represents later insight. The controversy is used to illustrate the misunderstanding between the religious leaders and the Jesus community. Official opposition has been absent for a while, but when conflict erupts it becomes a pretext for Jesus teaching again in parable form. He condemns Pharisaic profiteering and the small-mindedness of human tradition in contrast to the radical demands of scripture.

The related Old Testament reading picks up the demand of God's law, in contrast to mealy-mouthed compromise. A deity whose image can be held and manipulated by human beings cannot truly be God, so there is passionate hostility to any form of idolatry. When God revealed his will to Moses he was hidden in fire and no form was visible. The first two commandments are given added emphasis and are not open to change or modification. Psalm 15 reinforces the focus on social ethics as part of the worship of God and a condition for admission to the Temple.

The Letter of James was included in the canon of the New Testament late and with reservation. Martin Luther famously described it as an 'epistle of straw' because it says nothing about the death and resurrection of Jesus and, in his view, contradicts the true gospel of 'justification by faith' by preaching mere 'works'. It is a consistently ethical document and in this first chapter the author uses a principle used by other New Testament authors: if God is one, and the human person should be one – then our aim is to

110

imitate God in whose likeness we are created. Often the theme is 'the imitation of Christ', but James is not using a distinctively Christian form. For him and for his community Christianity is a way of life before God – representing a form of the Gentile mission independent of Paul's and not involving any radical disjunction from Judaism. What is at issue is the inconsistency of human behaviour, and the target is the would-be religious person who doesn't put it into practice.

The Old Testament reading from the Song of Songs – and Psalm 45, the Canticle – lift up the realm of earthly and profane things and see them as deeply religious. The Song of Songs is best viewed as an anthology of poetry – each poem loosely related to the others by the theme of human erotic love. This may be referred to in terms of divine love and of rituals celebrating the cycle of life and death. There is garden imagery, mutuality of relationship – as in Eden – even the suggestion of a female author. Psalm 45, similarly, has a profane lyric. It is a song of praise in honour of a young king and his consort – but was reinterpreted to refer to the Messiah and, in this sense, incorporated into the Psalter. The New Testament extended this to the relationship between Christ and the church.

★   ★   ★

Proper 18
(Sunday between 4 and 10 September)

Proverbs 22:1–2, 8–9, 22–23 *with* Psalm 125
or Isaiah 35:4–7a *with* Psalm 146
James 2:1–10, 14–17 *or* James 2:1–17
Mark 7:24–37

A SHARP contrast to the hostility of the Jewish authorities, of last week's Gospel reading, is supplied by the faith of the Syro-Phoenician woman in this week's. Mark follows the controversy over food with the surprising faith of a Gentile who comes

111

to Jesus. He has just challenged the basis of the levitical distinction between what is clean and what is unclean, and here tackles a second issue which was divisive amongst the early Christians. If 'cleanness' depends on our attitudes, then the distinction between Jew and Gentile will also fall. After this the cure of the deaf man – the first case to be reported – should probably be understood symbolically. The secrecy motif underlines that it is only those who believe in the risen Lord who can understand what is taking place. Just as Jesus restores hearing, so he gives the spiritual faculty to understand what is obscure to the disciples, who think they can hear but show by their behaviour how little they really understand.

The related Old Testament reading is part of the vision of restoration from Isaiah 35. The helpless exiles will return to Jerusalem, 'the ears of the deaf unstopped' as part of the hope of God's kingdom finally come. Psalm 146 is a hymn of praise to the Lord who 'sets the prisoners free' and 'opens the eyes of the blind'; a vision of trust and hope in God's power, similar to that in Isaiah.

In the second chapter James continues with his theme of consistency, exploring an attitude of discrimination between people at some length. Discussion of the relation between faith and works usually centres on verses 14ff., but the issues are there right through the chapter, set out firmly in terms of final judgment. Favouritism and faith are irreconcilable. James reaffirms a central tenet of Jewish teaching, namely that it is the oppressed and marginalized who matter most to God, and it is they who should matter in the community. Christianity is a way of life. It makes no sense to speak of 'faith' as though it can exist in its own right.

A selection of three readings from the book of Proverbs begins, this week, with an example of some of the one-liners from an early collection. These are presented as the instruction given by a teacher to a pupil in the royal court and reflect good homely wisdom with an appeal to ethics and common sense in the context of faith in God: 'whoever sows injustice will reap calamity'. Psalm 125 is a hymn of trust in God's faithfulness and a prayer for the security of God's people and the faithfulness of Israel.

★   ★   ★

Proper 19

(Sunday between 11 and 17 September)

Proverbs 1:20–33 *with* Psalm 19 *or* Wisdom of Solomon 7:26–8:1
or Isaiah 50:4–9a *with* Psalm 116:1–9
James 3:1–12
Mark 8:27–38

T HE second reading from Proverbs is addressed to a general
audience by a personified Wisdom. This is not, as last week,
a collection of single-line proverbs but a more sustained piece in
which Wisdom presents herself in the public places of the city,
addressing herself to 'simple fools' and delivering a speech in which
she rejects those who have refused to listen to her, but promises
security to those who submit to her guidance.

There is a choice of Canticles – Psalm 19 or the Wisdom of
Solomon. The Psalm itself consists of two, originally independent,
songs – and the lectionary gives the option of using only verses
1–6. This first part is a nature Psalm proclaiming the awe and
majesty of God revealed in creation (bearing analogy to Psalm 8)
whereas the second part (vv. 7–14) is on the theme of the law
and is not unlike Psalm 119. The two halves were then united for
use in public worship, the idea of a divine order (in nature as in
history) making the connection between them.

The Wisdom of Solomon is a Greek work by a Hellenistic Jewish
author, usually dated from 100 BCE to 100 CE on the basis of its
links with contemporary philosophy. This canticle is part of an
'autobiographical' section in which the characteristics of Wisdom
are delineated by 'Solomon'. He loves her like a bride, and it is
worth noticing the transformation she has undergone since she
was personified in our Proverbs passage. By now she is an almost
divine figure paralleled with Isis and designed to wean the educated
Jewish youth of Alexandria back to true Judaism and true wisdom,
away from the attractions and status of Greek culture.

The use and misuse of speech seems to be a real problem for the

113

author of James. One of his central concerns is about teachers, as demonstrated in our New Testament reading on the use of the tongue. The issue is not, as might be expected, that of false teaching. Rather it seems to be arrogance, gossip and the criticizing of others in the community, directly or otherwise. Probably to be a teacher or a rabbi carried its own sense of superiority, hence the strong impression that many people wanted to be teachers. So James spells out the responsibilities and dangers of the role and in this passage we see the heart of his concerns, including what he sees as the most important ethical issues. That is, to speak evil against one's fellow and to fail to live according to what one says are equally a denial of true Christian life, self-deceiving and incurring divine judgment.

The Gospel passage marks the watershed in Mark's story. It begins the way of the cross and at this half-way point we have a reiteration of the truth about Jesus's identity. The disciples' eyes are opened and from now on they will be taught the manner of their discipleship. This is teaching enclosed between two miracles of restored sight – symbols of their blundering efforts to assimilate and live by their learning. As Jesus predicts his death, so the atmosphere of the Gospel changes dramatically and the dominant theme becomes that of the cross. In Mark's context the crucial divide is not between those who acknowledge Jesus as the Messiah and those who do not, but between those disciples who are prepared to follow him on the way of suffering and those who are not.

The related Old Testament reading is the third Servant Song of Second Isaiah – a confession of confidence spoken by one commissioned to mediate God's word and understanding his task and sufferings as part of a prophetic task. The related Psalm is a thanksgiving to God for saving the Psalmist's life. He will now walk in communion with God, bound by an obligation to do God's will. As, in Mark's Gospel, Jesus's disciples turn with him towards Jerusalem, so they are similarly bound to learn the meaning of their task.

★　★　★

Proper 20

(Sunday between 18 and 24 September)

Proverbs 31:10–31 *with* Psalm 1
or Wisdom of Solomon 1:16–2:1, 12–22 *or* Jeremiah 11:18–20
with Psalm 54
James 3:13–4:3, 7–8a
Mark 9:30–37

T HIS final section of the book of Proverbs comprises a poem about the virtuous wife. It is written in the form of an alphabetic 'acrostic', which means that the whole Hebrew alphabet is used to begin each line in turn. The purpose of this device serves to reinforce the idea of the complete perfection of the woman – making a connection with the figure of Wisdom from last week's reading. This 'capable woman' provides a contrast with the 'strange woman' of the early chapters and the poem gives a positive conclusion to the book as a whole. Psalm 1 sets out the choice of 'two ways' (the way of righteousness and the way of wickedness) and calls for responsible obedience to God.

James too draws on the wisdom tradition and distinguishes sharply between the way of true wisdom and the way of folly. He perceives the major problem to lie with human nature and the human condition. True wisdom comes from above and shows its effects in action. It is the divided nature of the individual which lies at the heart of divisions in the community. He doesn't address the question of where evil comes from but implies that individuals can resist it from their own resources. James has final judgment within his perspective, stressing the urgent need for humility and transformation.

In the Gospel passage Jesus again foretells his death and resurrection, one of a series of predictions which dominate this section of the narrative and remind us of his inevitable destiny. The disciples characteristically demonstrate their inability to understand his words – and here they fail to see the implications for themselves either. Jesus responds by teaching them about the paradox of discipleship and the reversal of values in the kingdom.

The related Old Testament reading is to be taken either from the Wisdom of Solomon or from Jeremiah. The former passage is a discourse on the ungodly and their ways. It tries to expound the logic of the way the wicked think: that they were born by mere chance and destined for nothingness and must therefore live to enjoy the present moment, oppressing the righteous. But the message of the passage is that the ungodly are deceived. Humanity was created not for corruption but for immortality, and the righteous will ultimately be exalted.

The lament from Jeremiah reveals evil schemes directed against him and against the community. The image of a tree about to be destroyed with its fruit is used of the nation unaware that it is about to be slaughtered – and possibly too of the individual prophet threatened by a plot. What Yahweh is planning to do to the community Jeremiah's enemies are planning to do to him. The Psalm too is in the form of a lament for a man persecuted and threatened by death and violence who puts his trust in divine faithfulness but cannot quite endure the suffering patiently and whose own will retains its power in his prayers.

★   ★   ★

Proper 21
(Sunday between 25 September and 1 October)

Esther 7:1–6, 9–10; 9:20–22 *with* Psalm 124
or Numbers 11:4–6, 10–16, 24–29 *with* Psalm 19:7–14
James 5:13–20
Mark 9:38–50

DERIVING its title from the name of its heroine, the book of Esther presents the story of an unsuccessful attempt to kill the Jews living in the Persian empire in the fifth century BCE. The threat was averted by the courage and shrewdness of Esther and her cousin Mordecai. The two forces of destiny and human initiative are entwined in the message of the book. In the right time and place, human individuals can hold the destiny of their people in their hands. Since the story explains the origin of the festival of Purim, Jewish custom is to read the Esther Scroll on this occasion and to exchange gifts in celebration of national deliverance and the triumph of good over evil. Psalm 124, set as the canticle, picks up this theme in thanksgiving for the many acts of deliverance in the history of God's people.

Our final reading from the Letter of James concerns the prayer of faith for healing. This is a community of 'the word', where teachers have real status; but the impression given by the letter as a whole is that the author doesn't want any formal hierarchy in the church. He sees prayer as having a high priority for everyone, both individually and collectively, and wants above all to close the gap between what is said and what is done.

The Gospel reading continues Jesus's paradoxical teaching about discipleship. First, there is the narrative about the exorcist which seems to be included because it underlines the all-important distinction between being 'for' Jesus or 'against' him. It's a story which may reflect disputes where church leaders tried to exercise a monopoly in certain gifts. They are rebuked for their exclusive attitude. As in the wilderness after Sinai, so after the transfiguration/resurrection, the Lord's Spirit is not the property of a hierarchy. A collection of sayings about life and death completes the section of teaching. Its main theme is that of reward and punishment, reminding Mark's readers of the vital importance of their response to Jesus and to the gospel. On the one hand, there is the promise of reward and entry into life; on the other hand, there is the threat of losing that privilege.

The related Old Testament reading is from the Book of Numbers, a passage where confidence in a future in the Promised Land has been displaced abruptly by despair and the anti-climax following the giving of the Law. A series of complaint stories provoke various sorts of divine punishment, usually stopped by the intercession of Moses. Here the complaint is about having to eat manna, a disappointing diet after the meat, melons and garlic of Egypt. Moses, at his wits' end, is instructed to bring seventy elders to the Tent of Meeting. They will receive the Spirit and help him to carry the burden of the people. Two others also received the Spirit although they had remained in the camp – and Moses rules that they too may prophesy. The Lord's Spirit is nobody's exclusive property: 'I wish that all the Lord's people were prophets.' The second part of Psalm 19 is on the theme of the law. It praises the decrees and ordinances of the Lord: 'More to be desired are they than gold, even much fine gold.' On one hand 'the fear of the Lord, enduring of ever'; on the other hand the risk of 'great transgression'.

★   ★   ★

Proper 22
(Sunday between 2 and 8 October)

Job 1:1; 2:1–10 *with* Psalm 26
or Genesis 2:18–24 *with* Psalm 8
Hebrews 1:1–4; 2:5–12
Mark 10:2–16

THE next four Sundays in 'ordinary time' will include readings from Job and from the Letter to the Hebrews alongside the Gospel from Mark. This may provide an opportunity to do some more sustained thinking about these two often-neglected texts.

The Book of Job is an extended discussion of the question of suffering. It falls into the category of 'wisdom literature' and is hard to date more precisely than somewhere between the seventh and the second centuries BCE. It gives us a debate on the causes of suffering in which conflicting points of view are put forward, none of them presented as the final unambiguous answer. This makes it a stimulating read, given to us in the form of a good yarn about Job, his four friends and God. Today's reading sets the scene: the Satan challenges God's boast about Job as 'a blameless and upright man' – and God accepts the challenge. The decision is known to these two protagonists, to the council of heaven and to the audience – but not to the victim, Job. And so the narrator evokes our sympathy for him!

Psalm 26, set as the canticle, is also concerned with innocence. In the face of unwarranted accusation the worshipper looks for vindication in the Temple where he submits to the rituals of purification. His willingness to be faithful to God and his trust in God's grace enable him to stand firm, like Job, joyfully confident that his prayer will be answered.

The Letter to the Hebrews opens with the assertion that God has spoken his final word in the person of his Son. This emphasis on the uniqueness and perfection of the Son, in comparison with the imperfection of all others, remains the prominent theme of the book. According to today's reading those to whom it was addressed were being tempted to assign to angels a position above that of Christ, and were accordingly in peril of losing hold of their salvation (2:1–4). It was God's intention at creation that man (Adam) should exercise sovereignty on his behalf, as attested by the Psalmist. But Psalm 8 serves a wider purpose than just to establish Jesus's sovereignty over the angels. Here it forms part of the foundation upon which the author will present Christ as superior to all other divinely appointed means of access to God. His entry into heaven becomes the surety that 'many sons' will be brought to glory (2:10). Although the author of Hebrews stresses the supremacy of Jesus, he does not do so at the expense of his solidarity with the rest of humanity.

Those who follow Jesus are those whose aim is to do the will of God, not to look for concessions. Hence our Gospel reading about divorce is set in the context of teaching on discipleship. Since human weakness continues even within the Christian community, the possibility of divorce must also continue – but always with the recognition that it is necessary because of human failure, and never as an automatic right. Divorce is a spiritual and social tragedy in which issues of justice must not be lost. Both parties must have the right to take the initiative and both must accept the responsibilities and limitations involved in the death of a marriage. The section on children is included because it seems to follow thematically, but it is also about the meaning of discipleship – a reminder that the kingdom is given to those who are content to receive it as a gift, and a warning to those in the community who attempt to exert their powers inappropriately.

The alternative Old Testament reading (from Genesis 2) is directly related to the passage from Mark's Gospel, being primarily concerned with questions of equality, mutuality and companionship in creation. Psalm 8 relates to the New Testament reading and is a song of praise glorifying God the Creator. It enumerates the animals on the model of the same ancient cultic tradition as underlies the priestly creation story in Genesis 1.

★　　★　　★

Proper 23
(Sunday between 9 and 15 October)

Job 23:1–9, 16–17 *with* Psalm 22:1–15
or Amos 5:6–7, 10–15 *with* Psalm 90:12–17
Hebrews 4:12–16
Mark 10:17–31

JOB, model for sufferers though he is, does not remain in an attitude of acceptance for long. As the story progresses we meet a mind in turmoil, a sense of bitterness and anger, of isolation from God and even persecution by God. Here, in our second reading, a flight of hope takes hold and Job is ready to take the initiative and find God so that he can deliver his summons and press his case. His search for God reflects themes from the traditional quest of the sages for wisdom. He, however, is searching for God himself – not immortality, wisdom or glory. His goal is to see God and not merely to accept his unspoken verdict. Far from an affirmation of trust in God the speech closes with Job's cry of frustration and terror. Psalm 22, set as the canticle, is sacred to Christian memory because Jesus used its opening words in his prayer on the cross: 'My God, My God why . . .' As with Job, it is not so much the physical suffering as the anguish of mind which lays the Psalmist low and provokes his search for God.

The passage from Hebrews warns its readers against imitating the unbelieving Israelites in the wilderness in their disobedience to the word of God. Christ's superiority to angels, to Moses and now to Aaron is demonstrated. The establishment of Jesus's priestly credentials begins, suggesting that the writer may be countering some glamorization of the past amongst other Jewish sectarian groups. Heaven is depicted as the superior 'holy of holies' into which Jesus has entered and from which he summons Christians to draw near to God. It is not principally the earthly Jesus that readers are urged to look to, so much as to the Christ who has reached the goal for which they are striving. They are to be encouraged in their struggle. Following after last week's Gospel reading, the story of the rich man who could not abandon his possessions makes an intriguing contrast with the saying about those who enter the kingdom of heaven like children. Again Mark confronts his readers with the demands of discipleship. It was supposed that his wealth would make possible the young man's salvation, but Jesus's point is that it's not as easy as that. We don't submit naturally to what is asked of us, despite it being a prerequisite for entering the kingdom.

The related Old Testament reading picks up the theme of material riches. Amos weighs in against the injustices of wealth and poverty, reminding his hearers that God's judgment will fall on Israel for the sins of bribery and corruption which impoverish the needy. Those who feel secure in their material well-being will discover that their confidence is ill-founded. Psalm 90 considers the effects of God's wrath and prays for deliverance from such adversity. It laments the frailty of human existence and prays that people may learn wisdom from considering this, that Israel may be spared.

★　　★　　★

Proper 24

(Sunday between 16 and 22 October)

Job 38:1–7 *or* Job 38:1–7, 34–41 *with* Psalm 104:1–9, 24, 35c
or Isaiah 53:4–12 *with* Psalm 91:9–16
Hebrews 5:1–10
Mark 10:35–45

JOB'S great passion was to confront God face to face, though no mortal could see God and live. The shock ending to the story is that God does indeed appear – and does speak to Job as he did to the heroic figures of the past. But he does not confound Job with his 'terror' but with questions. The explicit theme of God's defence is that of 'design', developed by a treatment of all the major phenomena of the universe – fixed times and celestial laws – of which, nevertheless, paradox and incongruity are a necessary part. There is no simplistic answer to the problem of innocent suffering. God does not eliminate the forces of chaos but challenges Job to show some discernment of the constraints on his design. Job's complaint that the innocent suffer unjustly is never refuted. It stands side by side with God's answers as the demand for litigation is reluctantly dropped. Psalm 104, set as the canticle, reiterates the beauty and purpose of the world and the glory and wisdom of its creator.

In the Letter to the Hebrews Jesus is never depicted as the incarnation of a pre-existent being. Occasionally, as in this passage, the author suggests that Christ was appointed Son of God when he was exalted into heaven. He begins by setting out three ideal criteria for any high priest: his common humanity (sharing human weakness), his tolerant understanding of sinners and, thirdly, his appointment by God to the task. The passage then applies these qualifications to the high priesthood of Jesus – turning to his suffering as evidence of his genuine humanity and the source of his effectiveness in the priestly role.

The third prediction of Jesus's passion, which is not included in our Gospel readings from Mark, is followed by an incident which demonstrates the failure of the disciples to grasp his meaning and see the implications for their own lives. No sooner is the end in sight than the disciples begin to ask for a share in Jesus's future kingly power. Mark reminds his readers that Jesus is indeed going to be proclaimed king in Jerusalem, but that it will be through shame and crucifixion. There may have been church leaders with a similar attitude to that of James and John, seeing leadership in terms of status and privilege.

The concept of healing and victory through the vicarious suffering of 'the servant of the Lord' was embraced by the earliest followers of Jesus in their interpretation of his death. The Old Testament reading from Second Isaiah is unique in biblical prophecy and has been applied and reapplied from the days of Babylonian exile until now. While it can clearly be related to the suffering of Jesus, the 'servant' has long been a corporate image for the whole People of God and can connect with the real threat of persecution implied in the Gospel. Psalm 91 reinforces the promise of divine protection in every danger to the person who seeks refuge in God and places their trust in him.

★   ★   ★

Proper 25
(Sunday between 23 and 29 October)

Job 42:1–6, 10–17 *with* Psalm 34:1–8 *or* Psalm 34:1–8, 19–22
or Jeremiah 31:7–9 *with* Psalm 126
Hebrews 7:23–28
Mark 10:46–52

THIS week we come to the end of the current series of continuous readings and the end of 'ordinary time'. It may be a good moment to tie up some loose ends. Not that Job's final speech does precisely that, though it resolves the conflict between himself and God. Both parties seem to preserve their integrity, but this is interpreted variously. Some think that Job is being ironic – that his final confession is made 'tongue in cheek', some that this is his final rejection of a blustering deity. Others think that Job capitulates to the will of God, and still others – perhaps most – that he comes to a new understanding and affirms his faith with appropriate humility. Clearly Job's intellectual questions about the injustice of his suffering are not adequately answered, but he himself is in the end satisfied, as a sufferer, by his encounter with God. The message surely is that there is no unequivocal answer. There are some things about which we must be agnostic. The enigma of the cosmic design remains. The Psalm, 'O taste and see', was much used in the ancient church during Holy Communion. Although its thoughts are somewhat loosely connected, the Psalmist's conclusions concur with Job's: the true happiness of the godly life consists in the living experience of God and not in being spared suffering.

In Hebrews the resurrection and ascension of Jesus constitute the grounds for claiming that his ministry is superior to that exercised by the Jewish priesthood. His enduring work is not that of offering the sacrifice (that is the prerequisite of his entry into heaven), but of interceding on behalf of the people. Because of his sinless death he need make no further offering. He has already exceeded the sinlessness expected within the cult by his life of filial obedience to God the Father. The recipients of the Letter to the Hebrews are to stand firm under persecution and to strive after holiness in imitation of Jesus. Their goal is heaven – now shown to be superior in every way to the old order.

The Gospel reading is the last healing miracle in Mark's Gospel, the story of blind Bartimaeus, included as the finale to all the teaching on discipleship over the last few weeks. It stands in contrast to the preceding failure of the disciples and symbolizes the ability of those who have faith in Jesus to see the truth. Equally, it points forward to the incidents which follow. Jesus is hailed as Son of David – and then his messianic status will be demonstrated by the ride into Jerusalem, by his judgment on the Temple and by the conflicts through which he will clarify his identity as he moves towards the cross. An appropriate climax to this cycle of readings, the Gospel relates well to the passage from Jeremiah.

This is a poem of great joy celebrating the return of the Diaspora, reversing the fate of the nation in the past. Whereas the invading army brought death, this procession brings prosperity and sustenance. Those who follow in its way, like Bartimaeus and the reapers of Psalm 126, carry the promise of new life.

★   ★   ★

Bible Sunday

Isaiah 55:1–11
Psalm 19:7–14
2 Timothy 3:14 – 4:5
John 5:36b–47

THE readings for Bible Sunday put the testimony of scripture at the heart of community life. They give it a solemn authority which goes beyond either the written page or any other kind of human cleverness.

The saving word which God speaks to Israel rounds off an extraordinary collection and brings the prophecies of Second Isaiah to an end. This is the same image as that evoked in the Prologue where, in 40.8, 'the grass withers and the flowers fall, but the word of our God stands for ever'. The word of God calls the people out of exile and leads them to the new Jerusalem; this is a grand term encompassing all God's thoughts and ways, all the promises of salvation. The first part of the passage is a public invitation to the hungry and thirsty to be guests at Wisdom's table, where food and drink can be had without money. The second part calls on all people to return to the Lord for his pardon and mercy and the promise that his word will accomplish the rebirth of a nation.

The Psalm proceeds from a hymn in praise of the Law to a personal prayer of supplication in its final verses. Underneath a traditional form and solemn dedication formula seems to a lie a living personal experience which has brought this poem into the mainstream of Temple worship. The Psalmist is conscious of being protected by the Law and feels privileged to share in its blessings.

Timothy has followed Paul's teaching and his way of life. He has learnt patience, love and fortitude under persecution and now he is to stand by what he has learnt. He is to remember that he has known the scriptures since childhood and that these are able to make him wise for salvation. The time is coming, we are told, when people will not tolerate 'healthy teaching' but will gather teachers according to whim, unable to hear the truth.

Finally, the Gospel passage set for today is the last part of the discourse on the story of the paralysed man who was healed on the sabbath. The miracle serves as the basis of a dialogue about whether Jesus's claims are really substantiated by God himself. The claim that Moses 'wrote of' Jesus (5:46) is not one we can easily support. But John is not working from proof texts. Rather the authority of scripture lies somewhere much more fundamental. The argument is that the whole of scripture – the whole Mosaic teaching – reveals God and his redemptive purpose for humanity, and that this revelation is fulfilled in Jesus.

★　　★　　★

Dedication Festival

Genesis 28:11–18 *or* Revelation 21:9–14
Psalm 122
1 Peter 2:1–10
John 10:22–29

A DEDICATION festival offers the opportunity to revisit the history of our community and to pledge ourselves anew to follow God's call, heard through our forebears in faith, and given afresh to us in their story. The lectionary provides a choice of first reading. From Genesis there is the narrative which describes how Bethel, later such a famous shrine, came to be founded as a cultic centre.

126

A sense of place is often important to us as human beings. Knowing the story of the stone enabled later generations of Israelites to identify themselves with Jacob and to hold his promise as binding for all time.

The alternative first reading is the vision of the New Jerusalem from Revelation. The symmetry speaks of perfection, yet it is perfection rooted in part in human endeavour. On the twelve foundations are the names of the twelve apostles, the faint-heart anti-heroes of the Gospels. In this passage we are given some support for the idea that we are called to 'build the kingdom'. It is not all left to some millennial miracle. Human beings infused with the Spirit can contribute here and now to the future reign of God. The City is not simply a restored Garden of Eden, though it incorporates an unspoiled paradise. It is also a place of human culture and community, adorned with beauty, and sharing in the creativity of God.

The reading from 1 Peter turns to the nature of Christian community which the author outlines in terms drawn from the Old Testament. The basic image is of the people of God as the 'temple of God', the nearest which this letter comes to Paul's metaphor of the Body. Christ and Christians belong to the same community and are bound together in the same unit, Christ himself being the 'living stone'.

The central section of John's Gospel closes with a tense meeting between Jesus and the Jews. The question of his identity must now be given a direct answer. The passage set for our Gospel reading is all about the relation of Jesus to the Father – no accident that it was the feast of Dedication. The festival of Hanukkah commemorates the re-hallowing of the altar after its desecration by Antiochus Epiphanes. For the author of the Fourth Gospel Jesus's relationship to the Temple feasts marks the progress of his mission as revealer of the Father. Our religious practice is also judged by the extent to which it reveals God's glory in the world.

★　　★　　★

All Saints' Day

(Sunday between 30 October and 5 November)

Wisdom 3:1–9 *or* Isaiah 25:6–9
Psalm 24:1–6
Revelation 21:1–6a
John 11:32–44

A LL Saints' Day celebrates those who have gone before us in faith and reminds us of that to which we too are called. It is a day of high festival as we embark on the season of 'remembering' which lasts throughout the first half of November.

The twin themes of celebration and vocation ring through the readings, but the selection for the first reading offers a choice about where we put our primary focus. The author of Wisdom is appealing to his readers to seek divine 'righteousness' that is 'immortal' and the direction of our passage is towards the past. Those who have already died, 'the souls of the righteous', are in the hand of God. It identifies those who seek God's will as the truly wise, for they will reign with God for ever. It is this identification of righteousness with wisdom which is the characteristic feature. There is contrasting polemic immediately before and after our passage, probably against unbelieving Gentiles and against Jewish apostates falling under the spell of Hellenism (the book is dated between 100 BCE and 100 CE). The pattern is that of a writer familiar with textbook rhetoric, hence the vivid contrasts and rather heavy style. He has composed an apologia for Israel's traditional beliefs in a cosmopolitan setting.

The other option, the reading from Isaiah 25, is unashamedly forward-looking. This is the feast for the nations at the end of time when, on the occasion of Yahweh's enthronement, foreign pilgrims too will be brought into fellowship with Israel and with Israel's God. Often the tradition regards the pilgrimage of the nations from the point of view of the gifts they will bring or the services they can render, but here they will be welcomed as guests. This is the banquet to which all are called – a vision towards

128

which all can strive. Psalm 24, set as the canticle, relates well. It was probably part of the liturgy of the autumn festival when Yahweh appeared as King. The first two verses speak of his dominion over the whole earth, then verses 3–6 seem to be a liturgy designed to be used upon entry to the Temple and its celebrations.

The New Testament reading is from Revelation, describing a new heaven and a new earth. The consummation of all things, though it lies beyond what eye can see or heart conceive, is nevertheless compounded of the materials and choices of everyday life now. This is a final vision in which human limitation is transfigured and fulfilled.

The story of the raising of Lazarus is probably best seen as an allegory of the passion, death and resurrection of Jesus. Lazarus represents all humanity – individually and corporately – and so shows us that to which we are all called. Death is not the end because, even in their frailty and mortality, the saints demonstrate that Jesus is 'Resurrection and Life'.

★   ★   ★

The Fourth Sunday before Advent
(Sunday between 30 October and 5 November)

Deuteronomy 6:1–9
Psalm 119:1–8
Hebrews 9:11–14
Mark 12:28–34

T HE period from All Saints' Day to Advent Sunday has some-times been called the 'kingdom season', culminating, at the end of the Christian year, with a celebration of the Kingship of Christ. Today this is primarily expressed in Jesus's victorious confrontation with the Jerusalem authorities.

The Old Testament reading is intended to link thematically with the Gospel reading in which Jesus endorses the Jewish scriptures. In some respects Deuteronomy is essentially a book of education, and this accords with its own claim that its teachings must be a fundamental basis for the life and daily routine of an Israelite's home. God is the central theme – hence the opening affirmation of the Shema (v. 5) which asserts that God is one single God. He does not exist in different forms in different sanctuaries, nor is he simply the head of a pantheon. This is followed with the words 'And you shall love . . .' The sanctuary and its rituals can be no more than an aid towards the real transaction with God which takes place in the human heart. The opening section of Psalm 119, set for the canticle, reaffirms that the law of God, the teachings of scripture, contribute more to this inward contact than all outward practice of religion.

The New Testament readings revert this week to the Letter to the Hebrews and the language of perfection. All sacrificial victims had to be without physical blemishes if they were to be acceptable to God. So, as victim, Christ offered himself without blemish (v. 14). This comes within a section which argues that Jesus was the superior victim (vv. 11ff.), suggesting that this is more than a claim that he lacked physical defects. Rather he gained moral superiority in a death willingly accepted as obedience to the will of God. It is his filial obedience which makes Jesus the ultimate mediator. Almost certainly the subsequent doctrine of the 'sinlessness of Christ' had its beginnings in the twin images of 'sacrificial victim' and 'high priest'. But the readers of Hebrews are to be encouraged, by Jesus's entry into heaven, to imitate his faithful struggle with suffering and persecution.

Jesus appeals to the Torah in his answer to 'a question about the law', endorsing what the scriptures say. There is no conflict between the commands of God set out in the Books of Moses and the demands of the gospel. The challenge to love God and to love one's neighbour, once addressed to Israel, is addressed now to Mark's readers. We left the Marcan narrative on the eve of Jesus's entry into Jerusalem. This reading comes as part of his showdown with the authorities there and recalls earlier clashes with the Pharisees. It is really Jesus's very last confrontation with his opponents until he is arrested and prosecuted by them – and in it he silences them once and for all. Mark tells us that no-one had the courage to challenge him thereafter. With this declaration of 'victory' the drama of the Jerusalem conflict reaches its climax.

★ ★ ★

The Third Sunday before Advent

Jonah 3:1–5, 10
Psalm 62:5–12
Hebrews 9:24–28
Mark 1:14–20

As the Christian year draws towards its celebration of Christ's 'kingship', today's readings focus on the entry requirements for that kingdom. This week's Gospel, from the beginning of Mark, explores the idea of repentance as a condition for the rule of God. The Old Testament reading from Jonah – a tiny fragment about his successful mission to Nineveh – also offers an opportunity to give some consideration to the need for repentance, a theme which it shares with the Gospel. The continuous readings from the Letter to the Hebrews carry on with an exposition of the 'sacrifice' of Christ in relation to Israel's cult.

The Book of Jonah, something of an anti-heroic work, presents an unflattering, self-critical picture of Israelite prophecy. Jonah is reluctant, malicious, unrepentant – and, when he finally resorts to prayer, uses the occasion to accuse God spitefully. However, in the passage set for our reading, he is nonetheless a successful missionary. The people of Nineveh proclaimed a fast, put on sackcloth and repented of their sins. God was so eager to save them that even the wicked Ninevites could be forgiven. The message is that Israel too can escape God's wrath by turning from evil and evoking the Lord's pity.

The author of the Letter to the Hebrews has argued for the superiority of the new covenant inaugurated by Christ, over against that of the Mosaic Torah. Jesus now appears in the presence of God on our behalf. The claim is that Israel's cult did not achieve its intended goal, namely the removal of the barrier of sin. Had it done so there would have been no need for sacrifice to be constantly repeated. Readers of Hebrews are being urged to accept the death and ascension of Christ as replacement for the entire sacrificial system, now rendered worthless. Unlike the high priest Jesus is not forever alone in the presence of God. Rather he will return to gather the elect who will then accompany him into the sanctuary. To the commonly accepted Christian confession that Jesus is exalted into heaven (Psalm 110:1) this author has added the idea, from the same Psalm (v. 4), that his death and ascension can be presented in priestly terms, giving a message of encouragement to his readers, now on the borders of the Promised Land.

The heart of Jesus's teaching is the proclamation of the kingdom of God, and the Gospel reading begins with a summary of this. It is 'good news' but its arrival brings judgment as well as salvation. It demands repentance as well as faith. The expectation that God would finally establish his rule on earth is a hope expressed in many different ways throughout the Old Testament. The question of whether Jesus believed that the kingdom had in some sense arrived, or whether he was referring to an event still to come, is much debated – and the tension between the two ideas is found in all the Gospels and in Christian communities down to our own day. There are those who emphasize that the kingdom is about obedience to God's will and can be built on earth. There are others who argue that it will burst into history, bringing cataclysmic judgment and renewal. We do best not to make a hard and fast choice. Only God can bring the kingdom, Christians can only repent and prepare – yet, according to today's reading, it has already drawn near in the person of Jesus who is obedient to God and confronts us with the challenge to share his obedience. The theme of discipleship is prominent in Mark, and his readers are to identify with the first group who struggled to follow after the Master.

★ ★ ★

The Second Sunday before Advent

Daniel 12.1–3
Psalm 16
Hebrews 10:11–14, (15–18), 19–25
Mark 13:1–8

THE Old Testament and Gospel readings again address the theme of the kingdom, here the apocalyptic emphasis of a future cataclysmic act of God. But, far from endorsing over-enthusiastic millennial hype, the message is one which counsels calm confidence and preparedness – faith in God's ultimate rule.

The first reading is the final promise of resurrection from the last chapter of Daniel. This is a passage which can be dated to about 165 BCE, making it very late in the Old Testament. There will be a time of anguish, but a group within Israel called 'the wise' will be offered an extraordinary deliverance. They are to teach 'the many' that God is in control of history, has organized appropriate times and seasons and has assured his people of their ultimate vindication. Attempts to predict a timetable in the apocalyptic scenario are doomed of course, but Daniel can still teach us that history gains its meaning in the lives of obedience which enact the coming of the kingdom.

For the author of Hebrews Jesus's sacrifice was superior to the old system because it did not have to be repeated. The exposition of Christ as priest and victim draws to a close, and a new section addresses the implications of this for the Christian life. There is an exhortation to perseverance as Christians are encouraged to 'hold fast the confession of our hope without wavering'. They are to provoke one another to love and good deeds and to meet together regularly. Jesus's participation in suffering and death have made his the superior sacrifice, so that his followers too may approach the heavenly sanctuary by continuing to live faithfully as Christian people in community.

The reading from Mark 13 repeats the Gospel's persistent message that the path of discipleship involves suffering and that it is those who follow this faithfully who will be vindicated. It has two inseparable themes: the suffering of Jesus and his followers and the punishment of Israel and its institutions. This passage is directed at readers of Mark's own day (notice the use of 'you') who are being urged to be prepared for a long struggle. Rather than suggesting that the end is near Mark is discouraging over-enthusiasm and counselling calm preparedness, rather than action. 'The time is not yet.' Final judgment is not yet imminent. Be on your guard against undue excitement. But 'keep alert; for you do not know when the time will come'. We will all one day have to account for the effects of our decisions in the present.

★   ★   ★

Christh the King

(Sunday between 20 and 26 November)

Daniel 7:9–10, 13–14
Psalm 93
Revelation 1:4b–8
John 18:33–37

THE final Sunday of the year celebrates Christ the King and, with him, the vindication of God's people and of all the nations. Everyone (especially those who are oppressed, but who retain a sense that God is with them) will come to recognize how little jurisdiction any worldly authority really has.

The central message of the Book of Daniel comes in this first great vision of judgment before the Ancient One. God appears on his fiery throne surrounded by his court; the record books are examined and judgment is given. He then gives to the 'one like a human being' universal and 'everlasting dominion'. This is the figure, traditionally identified as the Messiah, who seems to lie behind the 'Son of Man' title in the Gospels. In this context he

134

also represents all faithful Jews: those who come through suffering and are finally vindicated by God.

The beginning of the Book of Revelation brings together two Old Testament texts which were highly significant for the first Christians. One was the reading from Daniel, which we have just considered, and the other is from the prophecy of Zechariah which gives to our New Testament reading 'all the tribes of the earth will wail'. Zechariah goes on to describe the opening of a fountain for cleansing from sin and the removal of all idols. This universal penitence and cleansing is assumed at the very end of Revelation when the nations bring their glory into the new Jerusalem. Jesus's final coming is not something separate from his first coming which ended on the cross. Rather, it is its consummation, for he is the beginning and the end of all things. This author shares the Old Testament hope that God will gather in all nations through the death of his Son and the witness of his people. It is their witness which is the main concern of the Book of Revelation.

For the Gospel we have, as in Daniel, a courtroom drama: the climax of Jesus's extraordinary encounter with Pilate from John's Gospel. In all four Gospel accounts Pilate begins by stating the charge in the form of a question addressed to Jesus: 'Are you the King of the Jews?' John alone replaces the short non-committal 'you have said so' with an important discussion on the meaning of his kingship. In this Gospel the Jerusalem authorities have tried to seize or kill Jesus several times and, in the face of this hostility, he has set the sovereign tone early on: 'I lay down my life . . . I lay it down of my own accord' (10.17). Similarly, the trial scene is more a judgment of Pilate and, within it, a narrative of the Roman governor moving from incomprehension to an extraordinary acknowledgment of Jesus's power. The Jews have charged him with treason, but Jesus is King of Truth. Finally, in a moment of terrible irony, the Jews will acknowledge Caesar to be their king in order to be rid of Jesus, their true King.

The Psalm set for the canticle is part of a collection dealing with the kingly role of the God of Israel. These seem to have been composed for use in connection with a Temple festival of God's kingdom. Here, his rule is based on his control over the powers of chaos symbolized by the waters of the sea. Just as God gives order to creation so, in the last verse of the Psalm, he is said to order human life by his decrees and to demonstrate therefore his reign in history as well.

Biblical References

The Old Testament

Genesis 22, 26, 36, 40, 42, 46, 50, 65, 66, 82, 87, 88, 93, 118, 120, 126

Exodus 12, 19, 30, 34, 41, 43, 45, 47, 60, 65, 66, 70, 86, 103, 108

Leviticus 29

Numbers 30, 45, 116, 117

Deuteronomy 24, 27, 86, 109, 129, 130

Joshua 108, 109

Judges 12, 47

Ruth 20

1 Samuel 23, 30, 47, 48, 86, 88, 90, 91

2 Samuel 8, 10, 12, 49, 94, 96, 98, 100, 101, 103, 105

1 Kings 19, 105, 106, 108

2 Kings 12, 22, 32, 37, 101, 102

2 Chronicles 12

Esther 116, 117

Job 60, 64, 91–93, 118–120, 122–124

Psalms 48

Proverbs 35, 65, 67, 106, 107, 111–113, 115

Song of Solomon 109

Isaiah 3–6, 9, 11, 13–16, 20, 31, 33, 34, 38, 41, 52, 55, 56, 58, 61, 65, 67, 72, 75, 84, 94, 111–114, 122, 123, 125, 128

Jeremiah 18, 49, 56, 100, 115, 116, 123, 124

Lamentations 64, 94

Ezekiel 65, 67, 73, 82, 90, 96

Daniel 79, 133–135

Joel 38

Amos 98, 99, 120, 121

Jonah 25, 33, 131

Micah 20

Zephaniah 65, 67

Zechariah 10, 11, 51, 135

Malachi 29, 51

The Apocrpyha

Wisdom of Solomon 18, 36, 94, 113, 115, 116

Baruch 65, 67

The New Testament

Matthew 4–6, 12, 13, 16, 17, 20, 21, 38, 45, 62–64, 79

Mark 4, 6, 3, 4, 22, 23, 25, 27, 31–35, 37, 40–42, 45, 51, 52, 54, 57, 62, 63, 65–67, 77, 86–91, 94–96, 98–101, 109–111, 113, 115, 116, 118, 120–123, 129, 131–134

Luke 4, 6–11, 13, 14, 16, 17, 29, 30, 45, 47, 48, 62, 63, 71, 78–80, 82

John 5, 4–7, 15, 16, 18, 19, 22–24, 27, 32, 35, 38, 39, 43, 45–47, 49, 51, 53, 55, 56, 58–65, 67–71, 73–78, 80–84, 99, 101–108, 123, 125, 126, 128, 134, 135

Acts of the Apostles 10

Romans 8, 10, 13, 24, 42, 65, 66, 82, 84, 85

1 Corinthians 3, 7, 23–25, 27, 31, 32, 34, 43, 44, 56, 57, 60, 67, 68, 76

2 Corinthians 34, 37, 38, 47, 48, 86–88, 90, 91, 94, 96, 97

Galatians 16, 17

Subject index